How to Be Happy in No Man's Land

HOW TO BE HAPPY IN NO MAN'S LAND

A Book for Singles

by

IVERNA TOMPKINS

with Irene Burk Harrell

LOGOS INTERNATIONAL
Plainfield, New Jersey

HOW TO BE HAPPY IN NO MAN'S LAND: A BOOK FOR SINGLES
© 1975 by Logos International
185 North Avenue, Plainfield, New Jersey 07060

The LORD *thy God in the midst of thee*
  is mighty;
he will save,
he will rejoice over thee with joy;
he will rest in his love,
he will joy over thee with singing.
I will gather them that are sorrowful
  for the solemn assembly,
  who are of thee,
  to whom the reproach of it was a burden.
Behold, at that time I will undo all
  that afflict thee:
  and I will save her that halteth,
  and gather her that was driven out;
  and I will get them praise and fame
    in every land where they have been put to shame.
And at that time I will bring you again,
  even in the time that I gather you:
for I will make you a name and a praise
  among all the people of the earth,
  when I turn back your captivity before your eyes, saith
    the LORD.

(*Zephaniah 3:17–20*)

To my mother

whose life, counsel, prayers, understanding, and wit taught me that my only responsibility when I failed was to get up and try again with God's help. Now widowed after more than half a century of marriage, she is an encouragement to all who know her.

Contents

Preface

One day when I was praying for a group to which I was to minister, I got a mental picture of thousands of women, all shackled, all bound together. And in a moment, suddenly I saw all those shackles drop off, and the women began to move about in freedom and joy.

In my ministry, I've been privileged to see it happen. Shackles of guilt, condemnation, failure, hopelessness, and fear have fallen off. I've seen new creatures born, new life begin. And then I've told the women, "Don't go back into bondage. Stand fast in that which the Lord has done. Don't go up and down on a roller coaster in your Christian life, but let the Lord take you from the highest peak, higher and higher. He came to bring you *abundant* life. You can have it—if you'll take it and hold on to it." I've seen that happen, too, to the glory of God.

When people began to suggest that I put into book form for wider ministry the essentials of what God had given me to share, I shrunk back. Me? Write a book?

I could never be a writer. I read a lot, and most writers make things so complex. Sometimes I read an article four or five times, trying to understand it. When I finally see what the writer is trying to say, it's so simple I can't understand why he took so many flowery words to try to get it across. I can say it so much quicker. I believe the Christian reader doesn't want to read fancy words, clichés, and superspiritual attitudes. He just wants to see a hope. He wants to see Christ in us.

Well, God knew I was *willing* for the message He had given me to be put on paper—but how? By whom? There was no way I could respond, "Lord, here am I; send me."

But the Lord in His wisdom didn't mean for us to do everything for ourselves. In First Corinthians 12, we read that there are diversities of gifts, but the same Spirit, that it is part of God's plan that we should need one another, and that He has made specific provision for "helps" in the church. When He sent one of these "helps" to me in the form of a writer/editor who could work with me to turn spoken messages into written words, this book came into being. I marvel continually at the way God works all things together for good to those who love Him, who are called according to His purpose.

Father, Jesus and I ask You that each reader of these pages will hear what the Spirit is saying to her, not what I think I'm saying. I pray that out of these pages will come the words of the Lord, that the faith You have given us shall be stirred and quickened, and that Your word shall be spoken expressly to each one.

Let all prejudice and preconceived ideas and plans and wishes be set aside as we pay attention to Jesus, the author and finisher of our faith. You brought us here together, Lord, in these pages, for Your purpose. It is for Your purpose that we open our channels of communication, and we share and we listen. In Jesus' name. Hallelujah.

There was no man that would know me: refuge failed me; no man cared for my soul. I cried unto thee. O LORD: I said, Thou art my refuge and my portion in the land of the living. Attend unto my cry; for I am brought very low: deliver me from my persecutors; for they are stronger than I. Bring my soul out of prison . . .

(Psalm 142:4–7)

1. No Man's Land —Aauugh!

What's wrong with No Man's Land? Aauugh!

What's right with it would be easier to tell. In No Man's Land, you don't have a husband to boss you around. You can do your own thing, be your own boss, act exactly as you please—except for meeting a few little inconsequential demands made by your landlord, your employer, the Social Security Commission, your neighbors, your kids, your cat, your oven that's *not* self-cleaning, your canary, the school board, the sanitation department, your doctors, your conscience, your relatives, your creditors, your book club, your well-meaning friends, your alarm clock, the PTA, the IRS, the SPCA, the NAACP, the ICC—

None of us are very free, are we? Even without husbands to boss us around. So what's so bad about No Man's Land—having one less guy to tell us what to do?

Well, but husbands do more than boss around. They're

handy for a few things—like taking out the garbage, laying down the law to the kids, shoveling the snow off the sidewalk, bringing home a paycheck, running interference against the world. And loving. They're handy for that, too. Nobody else can quite take their place for loving. Not legally, that is.

As a matter of fact, there's so much wrong with living in No Man's Land, being without a husband, that well— For instance:

There's no one to go with you to the theater to the late movie you're just dying to see (or to stop at the Dairy Queen on the way home for a gooey hot fudge sundae). Of course, you could always go by yourself—stop for refreshments, too—but you'd feel like an absolute nut, and people would think you were on the prowl. Even if nobody gave you credit for wrong motives, it's just plain not safe for unattached women to be abroad late at night.

There's no one—legitimate—to satisfy your yearnings when a beautiful romantic movie has stirred your deepest needs for total belonging to someone, when you need to be part of a passionate embrace you won't feel guilty about in the morning.

There's no one person to share everything with—toothpaste and all—for better or for worse.

There's nobody to share in the decision making about the really big things. Should I send the kid to this new school? Should I sell the house this year? Should I let Susie go to the slumber party? What color should I paint the shutters? Where should we buy our steaks?

All decisions, wrong or right, are your own fault, exposed for all the world to see—and malign your judgment. How we long for the safety of "Well, I really couldn't say. I'll have to ask my husband."

You have to be tough enough to lay down the law to the kids, to explain the situation to the bill collectors, to tell off the neighborhood nuisance in no uncertain terms— A man's just naturally better at some things, but there is no man in No Man's Land.

When the car develops that funny noise under the hood again, there's no husband with the brass to pretend like it's something minor (even if you suspect it's the transmission again) and keep the garage mechanic from taking you for all you've got.

Of course you have to call the plumber yourself. And, naturally, you panic. Will he overcharge you? Will he think you're trying to seduce him? Maybe you should invite a neighbor over, just to be there when he comes—if he ever does—so the plumber won't try to seduce *you*. If *two* plumbers come, maybe you should call the police before things get out of hand.

There's nobody automatically on the premises to take care of things if you suddenly have to go to the hospital for emergency surgery—or if you get called out of town for your grandmother's funeral. Who'll bring in the milk, get the kids off to school, pick up the laundry, pay the urgent bills?

In No Man's Land, there are higher taxes, indefatigable cupids with terrible taste in men, the boredom of being a bridesmaid time after time after time. The supermarket specials are always on the "giant family size" while the price skyrockets on the only size you can use up before it gets rancid, mildewed, or just plain succumbs to built-in planned obsolescence.

Your life is full of hurts, dangers, insecurities, and yet most of the married world, instead of trying to help, to cushion the hurts, to protect from dangers, to alleviate the rejection, seems to go out of its way to condemn, to point an accusing finger, to take unfair advantage, to lift a quizzical eyebrow. On top of all that, they have no time for us—unless they can use us to babysit or to stay with grandpa while they party.

Even other singles—people in the same boat—are less than helpful. Other widows remind us too much of our own loneliness and bereavement; other never-marrieds only mirror our own feelings of rejection; other divorcées reverberate with our guilt and failure. They had it made once, but they blew it, just like we did.

Where's the help for us then? There are a lot of us.

A recent newspaper report says that one out of three adult Americans is single. Twenty-five million of them are women —never-marrieds, divorcées, widows—living in this forsaken No Man's Land where nobody in her right mind would choose to dwell, a land where the bristling barbed wire of public opinion has barred us from freedom, where problems and propositions whiz like bullets all around us. In the midst of it, we can really *hear* the devil like a roaring lion seeking whom he may devour. And we're scared to death that we're next on his menu.

Even if we escape being eaten, are singles doomed forever to half a life, to wondering whether that's better than no life at all? Or is there an abundant life? Somewhere? Somehow?

A long time ago, Saint Paul cried out, "O unhappy and pitiable and wretched man that I am! Who will release and deliver me from [the shackles of] this body of death?" (Rom. 7:24 TAB). That's our cry, too. And some of us have found the answer he found.

I am a divorcée who has found the answer, just as Saint Paul did, and I cry with him, "O thank God!—He will!

through Jesus Christ, the Anointed One, our Lord!" (Rom. 7:25 TAB).

That deliverance, with its release from guilt, its forgiveness, its freedom, joy, and peace, is available to everybody who wants it, to whosoever will. Circumstances may put us in No Man's Land, but in Christ, we can be joyful there. Hallelujah!

The road to happiness starts from where we are.

There is none righteous, no, not one.
                                    (Romans 3:10)

Him that cometh to me I will in no wise cast out.
                                    (John 6:37)

2. Rejection—And Acceptance!

When my future son-in-law was ready to buy an engagement ring for my daughter Debbie, he asked me to go with him to the jewelry store to choose among the four rings he liked best. He wanted to surprise Debbie and needed my help. I just love jewelry, and so I was happy to accept his invitation.

When we arrived at the gleaming crystal and silver jewelry store, Randy didn't bother to introduce me to the jeweler, but just explained that we had come to pick out a ring. The balding, portly jeweler looked at me with obvious curiosity over the top of his glasses as I tried on the rings, holding my hand out at arm's length to admire each in turn and to discuss their relative merits with Randy. I oohed and ahhed over them all.

"Oh, Randy, I think this one is simply gorgeous—but still, that other setting is so stunning—and the cut of *that* diamond—look how it sparkles! It's so hard to decide which one I like best—" Suddenly I became aware of an uncomfortable disapproving look on the face of the jeweler. He wasn't shaking his head or saying, "Tsk! Tsk!" but he looked like he wanted to, and I realized what he was thinking.

It was too good a chance to miss. Looking him straight in the eye, I asked, "Tell me, sir, would you give me your honest opinion about something?"

"Yeah, sure," he said, temporarily forgetting his misgivings, and beaming all over as he set himself to recommend the most expensive ring.

Quick as a flash and with a perfectly straight face, I came back at him, "Do you think I'm too old for Randy?"

"Well—er—I—uh—"

I wish I could paint a picture of his face as it flushed from shades of pink to an embarrassed purple. When I burst into laughter, the obvious relief he expressed was all the answer I needed. We all laughed then, and I explained to him that I was the mother of the bride-to-be.

Just a few years earlier, such merriment would have been out of the question for me, because I was so bristly with defenses about my state as a divorcée.

Actually, I began my defensive role in life long before my marriage ever came unglued, long before I ever even met my husband.

In our day, a defensive attitude has become almost normal for anyone over twenty-five who has never married. This attitude is rooted deep in our subconscious. Remember how threatened we felt when we were little kids in school and the volleyball captains were choosing up teams? All of us just hated it. We'd stand there and look at the captains, and we'd try to persuade them, "Look, *I'm* really *great* at volleyball. Choose me." They always did, eventually, because everybody had to be on one team or the other, but when we were the last one chosen, time after time, something happened down deep inside us. And it began way before phys ed classes in grammar school. From the day we're born, there is a fear of rejection, a fear that we might not be chosen. And most of us never outgrow it.

Every unmarried is inevitably faced with the feeling, "Nobody chose me. I didn't quite make it. Somebody else was just a little more something—" (It isn't quite as bad for divorcées. Even though we blew it, we got chosen once.)

The feeling of rejection builds in us and takes its course, its toll, through our lives in a lot of different ways.

One common compensation for the feeling of rejection, of unwantedness, is listlessness. We just give up.

"I'll never amount to anything anyway. I was always dumb, always slow, I never understood math, and I was a lousy reader. They never chose me till the very last one for volleyball at school. But I don't care. I know the Lord loves me."

About a hundred years ago, I almost got thrown out of Bible school. A group of us girls put on long dresses, high lace-up pointed-toe shoes, pulled our glasses down on our noses, and walked through the cafeteria pigeon-toed, singing in shrill soprano, "No one ever cared for me, like Jesus."

Because we couldn't get a man, we had to go around defensively, advertising, "Nobody loves me." It was very funny to everybody—except to us. We were sick—we hurt—and we needed to be healed. We needed a positive acceptance of ourselves.

Sometimes the feeling of rejection expresses itself in unattached women through excessive drive. Some people drive to be on top of the social whirl, to run their friends' lives, to get an education, one degree after another. I have a friend who has doctorates in two different subjects, and she still goes to school perpetually, and works fulltime. She has blown the feeling of unwantedness into the drives of her life, and she just goes and goes and goes. She's a very attractive, talented, clever, astute individual—but still unfulfilled, constantly driven to make herself acceptable by outside accomplishments.

God doesn't want this from us. He has created us as we are. And if we are acceptable to God, we shouldn't worry about whether or not we are acceptable to other people. If God be for us, who can be against us? If people don't like us, that's their problem. They can nag at us, scream at us, yell at us, tell us we ought to get married, tell us how much better we'd look with ten pounds off—and it won't change a thing except *their* blood pressure. God doesn't mean for us to drive ourselves to be acceptable. He wants us to rest in Him. Whatever we are—if we're divorced, fifty pounds overweight—He has permitted it. And He accepts us exactly as we are; He doesn't wait until the new "improved us" approaches Him.

Acceptance of yourself—just as you are—is an absolute requirement for contentment. And genuine acceptance is not hedonism—the extreme of self-love and self-appeasement. The Lord doesn't want us to live that way, in love with ourselves in a sick, sick way. We're not to be pleasure seekers, pursuing what pleases us in the flesh. But we are to accept ourselves.

Recently, my daughter was talking with a woman who was always degrading herself, running herself down. Debbie said to her, "You hurt Jesus when you talk that way."

The woman said, "What?"

"Well," Debbie explained, "if you made a ceramic bowl and you brought it to me and I made fun of it, wouldn't you be hurt?"

"Naturally," she said.

"Well," Debbie went on, "God created you—just the way you are—and here you are complaining about it."

I made you just the way you are, and I don't want you to go around hating the vessel I made. I permitted certain circumstances in your life. I brought you by the easiest route you were willing to go, and I am working all things together for good. I'm using you just as you are.

In the light of God's revelation, it is sin for me to look at another person and say, "Oh God, I want to be like she is. She is so this and that and the other."

Don't deprive Me of My joy in the vessel I created. Learn to accept what you are. Learn to improve in the areas for which I've equipped you. Live in them fully for My glory.

In any gathering of people, there is a variety of personalities, a variety of emotional responses. We're all different, and we behave differently. Some of us worship the Lord with our hands up. Some worship Him another way. That's all right. The variety is beautiful. When we're together, and the Father looks down, He doesn't see a whole bunch of clay pots that all look alike. He says, *There's the one I made with the flower, and there's the one I made with the leaves. Don't they look beautiful together?*

As an experiment in self-acceptance, try taking the word "should" out of your vocabulary for twenty-four hours. You'll find you can't talk without saying, "I should." "I'm sorry, I should have changed tonight." "I'm sorry, I shouldn't have said that." Everything is "I should."

When we begin to genuinely accept ourselves, instead of saying, "I should be—" "I *ought* to be such and such," we can say, "I *am* so and so." This is not the same thing as self-tolerance. Self-tolerance is painful. Self-acceptance is release. Toleration is condemnation. Don't tolerate yourself. Accept yourself and enter into the joy of the Lord.

I think the Alcoholics Anonymous slogan should have been in the Bible. I don't know why the Lord didn't write it that way. I think it's fantastic. "God, grant me the serenity to accept the things I cannot change, the courage to change the things I must, and the wisdom to know the difference. Amen."

I carry that in my datebook. I have it in my Bible. I have it in my house. I have it in my car, and I trust that I live it in my life. "God, if there are things that must be changed, give me courage to change them, but help me to know the difference. Give me wisdom. Show me which is which."

Don't run around and compare yourself to somebody else all the time and say, "I wish I could be this." Learn who you are, what you are, and accept yourself as God has accepted you.

Often I find widows, divorcées, gals who have never married searching desperately for what they call their "place in life." They haven't accepted themselves where they are.

If you're one of these seekers, I've got news for you. You can stop looking for your place—because you're already in it.

Who says so?

The Bible says so. In Acts 17:26–27 Paul told the men of Athens that God "created all races of men [that includes us women] and made them live over the whole earth. He himself fixed beforehand the exact times and the limits of the places where they would live. He did this so they would look around for him, and perhaps find him as they felt around for him" (TEV).

Can you believe that God has put you where you are in order that you might find Him? It's true.

Later, writing to the Thessalonians, Paul advised, "In everything give thanks, for this is the will of God in Christ Jesus concerning you" (II Thess. 5:18). If we're to give thanks for everything, that includes giving thanks for everything about the state in which we find ourselves—"unclaimed blessing," divorcée, widow.

We don't have to go out swimming in some vast sea, saying, "God, show me my place." We're already in the exact spot, in the exact circumstance, He has designed for us. Our "place" is *where* we are this moment, *who* we are this moment.

But you don't like it? Well, that's okay, too. That He put you here for now doesn't mean He wants you to stay here forever.

Once you've accepted yourself where you are, who you are, He wants you to get on with the program, to grow up, to go from one degree of glory to another as you get to know Him.

But growth isn't something we can just dream about and *voila!* it happens. We have to do something, we have to set the growth machinery in motion.

Unmarrieds often think things are going to change just automatically. We have a tendency to think that what we're going through is just temporary, that we don't have to figure out how to handle the present, because someday, probably soon, we'll hear the clomp of the white horse, and our knight in shining armor will come riding through and swoop us up in his manly arms, crooning, "Oh, you're the one I've been looking for." And we think that when we recover from our swoon, we'll find that he's carried us away from all our unsolved problems to his castle in the billowy clouds where we'll automatically live happily ever after.

Well, we may not admit to dreaming *all* of that, but, in our minds, there is that "someday" fantasy that keeps us from facing and accepting our present situation.

"I really don't have to be successful at my job, because someday I won't have to work."

"I don't have to worry too much about what I am, because someday, someday—"

Such daydreaming has been a detrimental thing in our lives, letting days slip down the drain, one after another, with no progress. Not only does such "temporary" living keep us from the victory we're supposed to be experiencing today, but as the days go on and on, undealt-with problems pile like mountains around us. Inevitably, we begin to lose hope, and a woman who is hopeless is of all persons most miserable. We invite hopelessness when we place our hope in the unknowns, the maybes of life, the somedays that never come. We need to understand where our real hope is and head in that direction.

Singles who are separated but not divorced have an especially difficult problem of adjustment. You dare not focus too much on adjusting to the separation, because you and your mate might be reconciled in your marriage relationship. On the other hand, you have to avoid living toward the marriage that may never be again.

No one likes to just mark time. So don't. Use it for some inventory taking. As you discover areas of weakness, don't try to justify them. Correct what you can, accept what you can't correct, and leave the rest to God.

It's especially difficult for children to understand separation. The young ones sometimes cry for daddy or punish you with sullen quietness. The older ones demand explanations and offer immature solutions: "Why wait, Mama? Why don't you go ahead and divorce him and get married to somebody else?"

Your closest friends may be your most misguided "helpers." In their honest efforts to stand by you, they sometimes make belittling statements and insinuations about your spouse and try to fix you up with a date just to *show him* a thing or two. Other times they take the opposite approach, even offering their own seductive garments and candles for a romantic reconciliation over supper for the two of you alone.

Your attitude toward all helpers must be love, however unpalatable their actions.

Living in the complexity of separation and endeavoring to handle your own emotions without setting up unnecessary defenses, what is your proper attitude toward your husband? Should you compile a mental case against him, focusing on all past negatives? No. Such a procedure would give birth to resentment and nourish it into full-blown hatred. You have to realize that your husband is as confused as you are—even if he asked for the separation or caused it. He may have found someone else attractive and responded to her, but that doesn't eliminate the fact that he's been one with you and still needs you. It only increases his sense of guilt and failure, and makes him less able to make an immediate, permanent decision. If you understand this, you'll be in a better position to help him find the answer for his life and to respond maturely while he's still looking for it.

Surely your prayers during this painful period must be that each of you will discover what is important, that you will have the patience needed to wait for everything to be worked out, and that your marriage will be reinstated on a right foundation in Christ.

However temporary or permanent your No Man's Land status, hope has to be appropriated in the now. A long time ago, I was confused about this because the Bible says there is a hope laid up for me in heaven. I believed my "hope chest" was in heaven. It had my name on it.

I believed that when I got to heaven, God was going to give me the key to my hope. Everything I'd ever hoped and longed for was going to be mine. I believed that I was saved, baptized in water, and filled with the Spirit to endure till I got to heaven and opened my hope chest.

Then one day a minister said to me, "Iverna, if *I* believed that, I would get people saved, filled, baptized in water, and then I'd shoot them. There'd be no point in letting them hang around on earth any longer."

His abrupt announcement set me to thinking. I began to realize that there must be something for me in the here and now—before heaven. But where was it? As I began to search, I came to see that some Scripture verses I had projected way off into the future were applicable to today. And I even found a Scripture that said so: "*Now* you have every grace and blessing; every spiritual gift and power for doing his will are yours during this time of waiting for the return of our Lord Jesus Christ" (I Cor. 1:7 TLB).

I came to see that instead of looking to the unknown future, I needed to accept and look at the Right Now of my life and take a firm grip on the hope that is here. And when I began to do that, my life began to change, my joy began to fill up.

Forgiving one another, if any man have a quarrel against any: even as Christ forgave you, so also do ye.

(Colossians 3:13)

3. Condemnation—And Forgiveness!

One time when I was speaking to a Sunday school class, I made some kind of statement about how guilty I was because I had blown my life. The pastor heard about it and called me into his office.

"My, but you have a little God," he said.

"What do you mean?" I asked.

"Your God wasn't big enough to prevent your divorce or anything, huh?" he said.

"Well," I apologized, defending God, "I went my own willful way."

But he didn't buy that, bless him. "The Lord wasn't big enough to work in you to will and do His will, huh?" he persisted.

And right there, I began to get my eyes open. How many times, in how many areas, the Lord had worked in me and worked in me until my will was totally submitted to Him. Why, then, did I think He couldn't have worked back there?

I went to my knees and sought an explanation for why He

had let me go through all the ugliness of a broken marriage. "Lord, how come? Tell me."

Iverna, I supply all your needs, He said. *You needed this because you were so condemning of divorcées, remember?*

I remembered, and suddenly I understood. Before it happened to me, I had been death on divorce. I had a roommate in Bible school whose mother was divorced and remarried twice. Flatfootedly, I said, "I'm sorry, but I don't see how she'll ever make it to heaven. The Word says—" and I quoted all the condemning Scriptures I could think of:

"I say unto you, That whosoever shall put away his wife, saving for the cause of fornication, causeth her to commit adultery: and whosoever shall marry her that is divorced committeth adultery" (Matt. 5:32).

"Whosoever putteth away his wife, and marrieth another, committeth adultery: and whosoever marrieth her that is put away from her husband committeth adultery" (Luke 16:18).

"For the woman which hath an husband is bound by the law to her husband so long as he liveth; but if the husband be dead, she is loosed from the law of her husband. So then, if, while her husband liveth, she be married to another man, she shall be called an adulteress" (Rom. 7:2–3).

"And unto the married I command, yet not I, but the Lord, Let not the wife depart from her husband: But and if she depart, let her remain unmarried, or be reconciled to her husband: and let not the husband put away his wife" (I Cor. 7:10–11).

"Thou shalt not commit adultery" (Exod. 20:14).

And then, God forgive me, instead of quoting what Jesus said to the woman caught in the very act of adultery, "Neither do I condemn thee: go, and sin no more" (John

8:11), I spouted in my most prophetic tone of voice, "Be not deceived: neither fornicators, nor idolaters, nor adulterers . . . shall inherit the kingdom of God" (I Cor. 6:9–10). Then, while hopeless tears of anguish spilled down her cheeks, I painted for my roommate a livid word picture of the horrors of hell, the blazing lake of fire and brimstone which awaited adulterers in the second death.

It's a wonder my roommate didn't kill me. I deserved it.

The Lord, looking on my self-righteousness, must have said, *I see that Iverna's going to have to learn some things before I can use her.*

We all have to learn some things, and the Lord teaches us. He brings us by the easiest route we will come. Hardheaded and stubborn, I insisted on coming the most difficult way. Today, when I speak to groups of couples, and they ask, "Who are you?" I get up and say, "I'm a divorcée. I'm here to tell you what *not* to do. I know. I've done it. I blew my marriage, and learned a couple of things in the process. I'm sorry I had to learn them so painfully, but I'm ready to share what I've learned."

It's a marvel to me that I could have read that Corinthians Scripture so many times without noticing the very next verse where Paul speaks of the wonderful liberation, the perfect cleansing, that even adulterers can have through Jesus:

"Such were some of you: but ye are washed, but ye are sanctified, but ye are justified in the name of the Lord Jesus, and by the Spirit of our God" (I Cor. 6:11).

I guess my eyes were blind for a season, and I couldn't see past my legalism to embrace Jesus' love. In my humiliation as a participant in divorce, I finally came to see His attitude toward divorcées and received His forgiveness. Then I was free to forgive myself and to impart His forgiveness to others.

We can learn a lot about Jesus' attitude toward us by reading in John 4 about His meeting with the Samaritan woman. When she came to draw water, Jesus asked her for a drink. She was surprised, not only because Jews didn't usually speak to Samaritans, but because she could sense there was something unusual about this man, something pure, something holy, and she felt guilty about the sin of her own life.

Even before she opened her mouth and began to apologize for her own unworthiness, Jesus knew what was in her. He knew how she felt about herself. And He said to her, "If you only knew what a wonderful gift God has for you, and who I am, you would ask me for some *living* water!" (John 4:10 TLB).

(If *we* really knew Jesus, we wouldn't advertise our unworthiness either; we'd ask for—and receive—His worthiness and love. But if we've believed the lie that He doesn't love anyone who's been divorced, we don't ask Him for anything.)

As they continued to talk, Jesus began to create in her an appetite for that living water. "Whoever drinks of the water from this well," He said, "will be thirsty again, but whoever drinks of My living water won't ever be thirsty again. The water I give him will be like a well of water inside him, springing up forever."

The woman couldn't see any living water, she couldn't see anything with which to draw it; but it sounded so good, she asked for some. He had created in her a thirst such as she'd never known before, and she was willing to try anything. After all, with her life in the mess it was in, she had nothing to lose.

Then, suddenly, out of the clear blue, Jesus said to her, "Call your husband." He wanted her to know that He was aware of her situation; He wanted her to stop trying to hide her guilt, to acknowledge that she was a sinner—not so that He could shame her, because He didn't come to condemn the world, but so that, through Him, through His love, she might be saved and set free from all condemnation forever.

The woman answered in all honesty, "I have no husband."

"That's right," Jesus said. "You've had five, but the one you're living with now is not your husband."

(Imagine Jesus knowing everything in *your* life, already! And loving you so much anyway!)

Ouch! Jesus had exposed that sore place down deep inside her, the place she'd been trying to hide from everybody, because she had never *received* forgiveness. There was only one thing for her to do—change the subject. She asked a question about where was the right place to worship.

Jesus was all tenderness and compassion toward her, even then. He didn't say, "Listen, woman, you're skirting the problem." He told her that the *place* of worship didn't matter, that true worshipers would worship the Father everywhere in spirit and in truth.

And now she was beginning to get something. She said, "I know from the old writings that there's a Messiah going to come, called Christ. And when He's come, He will tell us all things." As she spoke, it hit her that this man knew everything. She asked herself, "Is this my Redeemer? Has the Messiah come? Is there hope for me?"

(Five-time loser and a present adulteress? No way. Maybe —by the skin of her teeth—she could make it into heaven. That's our attitude, isn't it? And that unfortunately becomes your own attitude about yourself.)

But when she said, "I know there's a Messiah coming," Jesus replied, "I am He." Then Jesus said to her, "I that speak unto thee—unto thee, divorcées, unto thee individually, personally—I know what you are, what you're doing, how you've been living— And you know who I am. I am *your* Messiah."

While she stood looking at Him, His disciples arrived, but Jesus never revealed her to the disciples. He revealed her to herself, unmasking her for her own sake. And she was able to lay her guilt down at the altar.

"Lord, I pour my soul out to Thee. Unto You, O God, do I lift up my soul. I can trust You. I can tell You anything, knowing You'll understand."

Jesus understood her feelings and He understands ours, because: 1) He was touched in every area of His life in the areas where we are touched; and 2) He made us. He's the clockmaker, and He knows how we tick.

Then the Samaritan woman went back to the city and said to the men—I don't think one woman in town would speak to her—"Come and see a man which told me everything I ever did." Of course, He didn't tell her everything, He didn't have to. She filled in the rest, just as when the Lord deals with me in one little attitude, I fill in all the rest of my mistakes. "O God, I'm sorry for this, and this, and this." I lay out every little nitty gritty thing.

He says, *Iverna, I'm concerned with your attitude. You can release yourself from guilt about these things. You know that your name is written in the Lamb's Book of Life, and when you can appropriate My very life within you, you'll have it made.*

All the laws that Jesus had given about divorce, He had given already when He met the woman of Samaria. I know that He loves me, that He has set me free, and I don't have to know why.

Too many of us divorcées keep setting ourselves up for rejection all the time. We mope along. The minute that little sore spot in us is hit, we go down, low.

In the church, they don't choose us to be teachers because we're so in and out, so up and down, and they can't trust us to be faithful. We're too touchy—somebody made some innocent remark to us, and we got our feelings all hurt, and went off on a tangent, reading into it more than they meant. It's easy for us to do that, because we are living failures. And every person in Christ had to come to the position of "I am a living failure" in order to pray, "God, be merciful to me, a sinner."

You'll never experience the happiness of abundant life until you have let Jesus deal with your failure. Jesus died to free you from all your scars, guilts, and sense of worthlessness. Holding onto them is sin—it separates you from God. When you feel separated from God, you don't worship Him. Satan knows this, and because he is out to get the worship for himself, he attempts to keep you feeling condemned. When he withdraws even one little member from church worship, he has gleaned a victory.

It's so easy to get rid of the scars, the guilt, and the sense of worthlessness that many people don't believe it. When you say, "Lord, I'm sorry. Please forgive me," He forgives you. Just like that. Seventy times seven. For promiscuity, dope, being five times married, living in sin. And when you turn from your wicked ways and look toward heaven, He doesn't only forgive you, He says, "I cleanse you from all unrighteousness. It's over in heaven. You're as good as new." That's all there is to it.

Many people say you haven't really been forgiven if you haven't forgotten. That was a source of guilt for me through the years—how *could* I forget?—until the Lord showed me that *He* was the only one with a capacity to choose not to remember.

The scars in my own life are there because of the sins I've committed in my life, and I remember doing them. Every time I used to get ready to worship the Lord, I remembered them the more vividly. About the time I was in spiritual victory, all of the nasty old gunk from the past would race through my mind—in technicolor. Usually, I didn't even blame the remembering on the devil, because I did a pretty good job of remembering on my own. And oh, the condemnation!

"Iverna, you're not worthy to worship," I'd tell myself. "You're not worthy to preach, you're not worthy to teach a class, you're not worthy to sing a song, you're not worthy to be in the choir. You're not worthy to walk in the building— Why, anybody from your past could come in and point an accusing finger at you."

I'd have to agree with myself. "Yes, it's all true. I'm not worthy—never have been. Why, way back when I was a little girl—"

Things that happened to me as a child are still affecting my life. Yet it's possible to be renewed, Saint Paul said. The inner man needs to be renewed daily. Now, there's no way I can go back into my subconscious and pull out all the things that could be affecting me. I can't do it myself, and I can't afford to have someone else analyze me at forty or fifty bucks an hour just to tell me I've got a problem. But I have a Lord who created me and who has had His eye on me all my life. He knows what's wrong with me.

I can pray, "Lord, I'm asking You to renew my inner man daily. Show me my subconscious hangups and why they're there. Literally move them from my subconscious to my conscious mind. Place them in front of me. Show me what causes what." As I have prayed this way, God has revealed me to myself in ways that have been amazing—but never condemning.

"Lord," I said, "You've never shown me anything to produce guilt. Therefore, You must be ready to deal with it in me." I'm not perfectly whole yet, but I'm a lot closer to wholeness than I was fifteen years ago when I began to pray that prayer.

We all have to begin to invite Him to deal with us, because the Lord is saying, *Listen, Church, I'm coming soon. And I'm coming for a Church without spot or wrinkle. Hurry up and get well. Accept My healing for your emotions, for your subconscious.*

You have scars, and some of you have adhesions on your scars. You drag them around from place to place, so touchy that you look like a bunch of grouches. You see the negative in everything, and your spots and wrinkles are growing.

Jesus must look at us sometimes like He looked at Jerusalem, saying, *I am the way, the truth, the life. Change your mind, people; the kingdom of heaven is at hand.*

But they paid no attention to Him. And He went out and looked over the city and said, *Oh Jerusalem, Jerusalem, how I want to gather you under My wing. How I want to draw you unto Myself. Oh, if you could have known what I wanted to do for you, Jerusalem. If you could have known I came for you.*

I think the Lord looks at us with compassionate love and says, *You who've been hurt, you who've known loss, you who've known failure, you who've known sin, you who feel you were never chosen—all of you—if only you could have known what I would have done for you, if you would have just received Me and appropriated Me into your lives. But you would not. Instead, you held to your own guilts and scars and remorses. And you decided that if you could not forgive, neither would your Father.*

But that's a lie. If you'll give it out, if you'll forgive others, not only in words, but if you will act love to those who have done despite to you, I will grant unto you mercy, and you will have it abundantly, and you'll be able not only to forgive others, but you'll be able to forgive yourself and to receive My forgiveness.

If we refuse to confess our sins, He can't pardon us. To sin is to miss the mark, fail to hit the bullseye—and who hasn't? So we confess it, He forgives us, and in forgiveness is freedom! After we have given everything to the Lord, we don't need to feel condemned anymore. We won't have to apologize, to try to justify ourselves, or to blame other people. We're free! We can say, "Yes, I'm divorced. O my God, I missed the mark. I just blew it. But the Lord has forgiven me. Hallelujah!"

Not only does God take the negatives of our life and weave them into a beautiful tapestry of living for us, but He teaches us that because He does this, we also can do it.

I saw the truth of this dramatically illustrated some years ago when I was counseling unwed mothers. One of the hardest times for these girls came when they began to experience the movement of the baby within them. They went through mental anguish, the whole gamut of turmoil and guilt.

"Here's the baby, he's alive within me, I don't know whether to keep the child—" All the frustrations, all the guilt, all the scars, came to the surface. I prayed, "O God, help me to know what to say to them." And the Lord gave me an answer.

I told the girls, "When your baby moves inside you, it's the greatest thing that ever happened. You have an ace in the hole, an advantage. Every time you sense life within you, instead of letting it be an occasion for re-awakened guilt and self-pity, let it remind you to say, 'I've been forgiven!' And then you can begin to praise the Lord."

As they did this, girl after girl came into victory. Every time the child would move within them, they'd say, "Oh, hallelujah!" realizing that the Lord had set them free. What had been a bad thing became a positive thing in their lives when they used it in that way.

I, too, have had to walk this walk. Every time memories of the past came to me that would throw me under, I had to say, "Hallelujah! Thank You, Lord," and He would turn my mourning into dancing.

When I'm traveling, I often see people from my past. The first time I did, I went into sheer panic. The people knew my ex-husband, they had heard stories about us—and here I was, standing up preaching the Word of God in church. When they walked in, I recognized them, and their eyes about popped out at me. I could read their minds: "Her? Iverna Tompkins preaching? Now I've seen everything!"

"This is it," I groaned. "Where's a trap door? O God, strike me dead right now." But my reaction lasted only seconds. Almost immediately, the Holy Spirit rose up within me, giving me boldness. I looked right at them and kept on preaching, and they couldn't stay in the face of that. They left before the service was out.

It takes that one spark of effort from you first. I don't know why, but that's the way faith works. The Lord said, "If you'll take one step, Peter, I'll be right there, bearing you up. One step of faith. But if you take one step into defeat, you're on your own. That's where you're going to live."

"Thank You, Lord. Oh, hallelujah! Lord, thank You that that man's shaving lotion reminds me of my ex—such a little thing (I've warded and steeled against the big things), but Lord, I'm not going to let that get me. I choose to praise You. I'm free from all guilt about everything, things I did wrong and things I could have done that I didn't do. You've forgiven me." No longer do I say, "Oh my God, if only—" but, "Thank You, God, that thing is over. Hallelujah. And Lord, I gave it to You, and I want You to keep it."

It's not enough for us to receive this forgiveness for ourselves. We have to forgive others if we're going to enjoy abundant life.

It's not too difficult for me to forgive someone if I'm convinced they've acted in ignorance. Anyone can make a mistake—seventy times seven times. However, once I've pointed that out to them and forgiven them and attempted to begin a new relationship, I don't expect a 491st time around.

Several years ago, a businessman offered me a working partnership which meant a move to another part of the country. The investment required on my part was small, and I accepted eagerly. It looked like a good deal. I applied myself diligently to the business, and was quite successful. Neither of us was taking salary or commission at first, but plowing what we earned back into the business to build up its capital.

After a few months' time, my savings were depleted in living expenses, and I decided to approach my partner about drawing a regular salary. Arriving at the office early one Monday morning, I was confronted with a startling and ugly reality: He had taken off for Timbuktu with everything I owned. And that wasn't the worst of it. I soon learned that house payments—and my car payments—that were to have been kept up by the company had not been made.

"Repossession" had been only a word to me before, but for a nightmarish few days, it became a reality. The children and I stood watching (like a scene from Little Orphan Annie) as the finance company towed the car away, and we looked on in befuddlement as men came to measure the size of the rooms in our house in order to write a For Sale ad for the newspaper.

In the months that followed, I grew bitter. I took great delight in telling my "poor little me" story to other people who were willing to share my indignation and pamper my self-pity.

One day I was sitting in church, consumed with bitterness as the congregation sang, "Pass Me Not." As I left the auditorium and headed for the exit, I stopped at the prayer room where I'd spent many glorious hours in the past. Without exactly deciding to do it, I found myself standing at my usual place of prayer. I could hear the congregation singing, "Heal my wounded, broken spirit; Save me by Thy grace." In an almost mocking tone, I said, "Yes—do heal my wounded broken spirit."

As the insincere words came from my mouth, I fell to my knees and began to weep. In the hour and a half that followed, the Holy Spirit purged that bitterness and replaced it with a genuine love and understanding.

Such victory! I could hardly wait to contact the man who had wronged me, and tell him he was forgiven. He hadn't meant to hurt me, he said. He had intended to pay me back when he made it big. But he had gambled and lost. There was nothing for him to repay with. But it was all right between us. The forgiveness was real.

Some years later, I decided God didn't really want women in the ministry, and so I resigned the church to re-enter the business world. The same man came forward with an offer of employment. I accepted and again worked diligently. He was pleased—and I was, too—for six whole months. Then I began to hear things that made me suspicious. I tried to get some of our verbal agreements put into writing so that my interests would be protected this time, but he kept putting me off.

History repeated itself. Overnight he was gone, the business was closed, and once again I was left holding a very empty bag.

For days afterward, I sat and stared. How could he do this to me? Twice! Somehow I couldn't even hate openly. I was crushed—broken in spirit and totally defeated. Then one day while I sat staring, the Lord reminded me of the words of a song He'd given me: "Take all I am or have or hold; Give me eyes that may behold my king, my Lord, my Love, who's everything to me." A final "Amen" to Him resulted in my returning to the ministry, with peace instead of bitterness in my heart.

I thought the problem was over until someone brought me word that God had gotten ahold of this man, and a transformation had taken place in his life. At first, I couldn't believe it. And I was appalled when I realized that I hoped it wasn't true! Why should anything good happen to him? I protested.

Once again the internal battling took place. The Lord showed me how I'd lived in violation of His righteousness time and time again, and how each time He had clothed me with His Son Jesus. Finally I asked for His grace with which to forgive—one more time.

One motive for my forgiveness was selfishness. I couldn't afford to pay the price of bitterness. For my own sanity and health, I had to forgive. The measure I gave would be the measure I got.

"If ye forgive men their trespasses, your heavenly Father will also forgive you: But if ye forgive not men their trespasses, neither will your Father forgive your trespasses" (Matt. 6:14–15).

You can't ask God for something you're not willing to give. Once a woman told a lie on me, something I could not disprove, and it went rampant through a church in which I was working. A couple of years later, she telephoned me and said, "I won't come to your home, and I won't go to your church, but I need to talk to you." I went to a coffeehouse to meet her and she said, "Because I spread malicious gossip about you, I can't grow spiritually. I'm asking you to forgive me, but I won't make it right with other people because of my own reputation."

As I was driving home, just swimming in indignation and self-pity, the Holy Spirit said to me, ever so gently, *Iverna, I have forgiven you of more than you've been accused.* Suddenly, I saw what I was doing. My attitude was "Poor, poor me," but the Lord showed me that whether or not that woman ever made this right, He had made it right.

Just as He sees us as a new creation in His forgiveness, so we must see the one we forgive as a new person.

How can you do this impossible thing? You do it by declaring out loud, "I forgive So and So." And you keep on saying that until your heart agrees with your mouth. That's faith in action. Then you can say to So and So, "I forgive you. I will praise Him." And I begin to praise Him through clenched teeth until my heart agrees. "I will forgive him. God, I forgive every lousy, dirty, rotten thing—all the times he cheated—" Let it all hang out. And there will come a time when you'll realize that a double portion of mercy has been imparted to you. And instead of forgiving through clenched teeth, you'll realize, "God, I didn't know I could love like this!"

The first time my ex-husband brought his wife to my home, I thought I would die. It was Christmas time, and he wanted to visit with the children. All day long I sang, "This is the day the Lord has made." When it was time for their arrival, I was totally calm.

As the car drove up, I walked to the door, and I remember saying, "Lord, please, it's got to be You."

When I opened the door, they stood there all dressed up. They'd just been vacationing, bought a new car, were on a second honeymoon, and when I opened the door, *I could have hugged them both!* The love of the Lord just absolutely poured through me, and they were far more scared than I was. My ex introduced me to his new wife, and I said, "How do you do. I want you to know that you are very welcome in my home." Honestly, I meant every word of it—but it wasn't Iverna.

Now I'm not saying something theoretical to you. This thing works, it really works. All we have to do is reach up and get it. Forgive. Receive forgiveness. Live!

Yea, though I walk through the valley of the shadow of death, I will fear no evil: for thou art with me.

(Psalm 23:4)

4. Fear—And Freedom!

In a strange city, far from home, I went to my hotel room one night, utterly exhausted from many consecutive hours of ministering. It was an old hotel, one whose doors didn't automatically lock when they were shut. But in my weariness, I forgot that. All I could think about was how wonderful a bath would feel, and then I could collapse in bed.

As I came out of the bathroom, I saw the door of my room opening. In lurched a man with bleary eyes, an unsteady gait, and a positively lecherous expression on his face. He shut the door firmly, and leaned against it. I didn't listen to what he started to say, but I interrupted, pointing my finger at him. Without being aware of any sense of fear, I spoke authoritatively—"Mister, you're going to get in trouble. You get out of here! Now!"

He looked at me for a brief moment, saw that I meant business, and turned to go, mumbling something about not meaning any harm.

After he had gone, and I had securely locked the door against any further intruders, panic swept over me. What if my bluff hadn't worked? What if—

But it had. And there was no need for me to be afraid. The Lord was my protection. I got into bed and enjoyed a refreshing night's sleep.

Singles in No Man's Land are frequently subject to fear, both of physical violence and the even more frightening fear of the future.

One fear that used to plague me after my divorce was the fear that I'd die before my children were grown up. This fear was a part of everything that happened to me. The flu became cancer, every cold was pneumonia, a sudden stop on the highway to the tune of screeching brakes was a fatal accident. These fears persisted, coloring every untoward event with a funereal pall until the day I heard myself pray, "Lord, You gave me these kids, and I believe You're going to allow me to raise them."

An affirmation of faith is the only route to dismissing other fears in our lives. Instead of worrying, "What if—" we need to say, "The Lord is in charge of my life. He is all-powerful. Nothing can happen to me unless He permits it to happen. And if I'm wiped out, then He'll provide for my children in another way. He'll never leave them or forsake them."

Gradually I have come to understand that there's no need for me to fear anything—in death or in life. I have put God in charge of my life, and I can surely trust Him to take care of every phase of it.

A widow must accept death, with all of its awesome finality, all of its mystery. It's hard to do. There just doesn't seem to be anything within us capable of doing it.

Many of us grew up praying, "Now I lay me down to sleep. I pray the Lord my soul to keep. If I should die before I wake, I pray the Lord my soul to take." We've automatically accepted the implied concept that if there's one little unconfessed sin in our lives when we die, we can't go to heaven.

When all of a sudden a loved one is taken from us in death, the scary question comes to our mind, "I wonder if he really knew the Lord. I wonder if there was any unconfessed sin in his life." And because we are afraid to consider these things, we shove them aside. We don't want to look at them.

The feeling is natural—and unhealthy. You must not hide anything from yourself. Bring this thing out into the light, let yourself be set free from this fear, so you can know security.

It is very, very rare that a person's life is snatched from him without seconds of last-moment breath. Instantaneous death seldom happens. For almost everyone, there are fleeting moments of last-minute awareness.

In a crisis, your mind can go through a thousand things in seconds. Maybe you've had the experience of driving along in your car, and suddenly you see another car coming right at you. You see there's no way to miss it, and in that instant, your whole life passes through your mind. You see it all in seconds—swish, swish. Then, somehow, mysteriously, it's all over with. The other car is gone, and you're still traveling down the road in yours, and you fall apart inside. "Oh! Thank God. I'm still alive!" But in that moment, those few seconds, your whole life happened before your eyes. Maybe you have to pull off the highway until you can stop shaking.

That experience is hope for widows who have feared that their husbands didn't know the Lord. The chances are very good that in his last fleeting moments, even when he couldn't speak to you, even when he didn't seem to know what was going on, there came the opportunity for him to embrace the Lord for himself.

I'm not trying to give you a false hope, but a real one. Our Lord knows who belongs to Him, and if anybody wants to be His, nobody can keep that person from knowing Him, no matter how up and down and rocky his life might have been.

Once I had a young man in my church. He and his wife had problems, problems, problems. I had counseled them on a number of occasions. One morning at seven o'clock my telephone rang. A woman's voice on the other end of the line was screaming hysterically, "They're trying to tell me Gene is dead, but I know it's not real!" Finally a man's voice took over. "This is Sheriff So and So, are you her minister?" When I told him yes, he described the accident to me.

The young man and his wife had had a real powwow the night before—a Christian fight. The next morning when he got up, they were hardly speaking to one another. He slammed out the door and got into his car to go to work. A few miles down the road, he had a head-on collision with another car. By the time his wife got the report, he was already dead.

You can imagine the fear that rose up in her mind, all the guilt that she picked up. "I caused his death. He's probably in hell—we won't be together in heaven." In the midst of their marital problems, he had exploded in vehement feelings from time to time. When you're angry and frustrated toward your spouse, you say a lot of stupid things that may not depict what you really are at all.

I knew what was going through her mind, and I began to pray, "God, give me wisdom."

I do not believe in false security. If a thing is black, I don't try to paint it white. If something scares me to death, I don't pretend it's okay. But I don't believe in false *in*security either. And as I prayed, "God, help me to know," the Lord took me back to some conversations I'd had with this man, times when he and I had shared the beauties of the Lord.

And the Lord began to remind me that this man *did* know Him. As he was driving along and looked up and saw the other car coming, straight at him, in his lane, what do you suppose he thought about, what do you suppose he did?

"Jesus."

In one moment, one word, "Jesus." If his heart was crying, "Be merciful and forgive me," the thing was done. You can take hope and faith in this. Our Christian hope is not limited to what we experience in this life. It is hope for hereafter, too.

What about those who were never interested in the Lord? You have to leave this with the Lord. But don't be afraid about them, either. The Bible says the Lord knoweth them that are His, and if they were destined to be His, if they were of the sheep that are of His pasture and He hadn't called them already, maybe He did in their dying moments. No man is in heaven or hell because of you. You don't have that kind of power over anyone's life.

Jesus said, "No one can pluck mine out of My hand." Maybe you made life miserable for your husband in the here and now, but you couldn't have consigned him to hell in the hereafter.

The enemy is such a cowardly, sneaky fellow that he tries to come in at your most vulnerable door. But the Lord says, "Neither do I condemn thee."

Widows also have to face the why of death. Some have had good marriages with good Christian guys, and all of a sudden they are gone into the unknown. There comes a cry

Godward, a fearful cry that carries with it a note of bitterness. "Why, God, if You love me so much, why would You do this to me?"

In my eyes, my dad was almost a saint. We had a very close relationship. We understood each other. Dad and I would talk like a couple of idiots. Neither one of us ever finished a sentence. I'd say, "You know that thing—"

He'd say, "I know, it just really—"

And I'd say, "I know what you mean." We just kind of knew where it was at with each other; we understood each other's thoughts before they were expressed.

If it had been up to me, I would have given dad a good strong healthy body and said, "You worked all your life setting up churches and building them and getting them out of debt and moving on. Now I'm going to reward you with retirement years in which you can enjoy the best this world has to offer." I would have done that because in my limited knowledge, that's the best I would have known to do for him.

But the Lord took him home to a better reward. It was hard for me, but I'm not afraid for him or me, because I know the One who's in charge of everything.

It would be ridiculous for me to try to tell any widow, "The reason the Lord took your husband is—" Nobody knows the reason, but if you will receive release, you'll be able to say, "Lord, I'm sorry I've been mad at You because You are God and You didn't *have* to take my husband. But I see now that You are supreme. It's beyond my knowledge. And I thank You, Lord, because I know You'll bring good from it—good for him and good for me. Lord, I trust You with my husband, and I trust You with my life. I'm not angry with You or afraid anymore."

I know what it is to want to die. Many people have

considered death as a form of escape from an unbearable situation. When you reach the depths of despair here on earth, you figure it can't be worse on the other side.

But the Lord says, *No. Life and death are in My hands.* When Jesus came forth from the dead—when He arose—He carried the keys of death, hell, and the grave. Satan no longer has the ability and the power to cause death. It is in the hand of the Master.

Just a month before my father died, he said, "You shouldn't see me like this, because this old body is nothing." He was a great big strapping guy, over six feet, and he had just wasted away to a shadow. He told me that he saw a lot of decrepit old bodies coming through the valley of the shadow of death, and at the end of it was a huge rainbow-waterfall— he didn't know which to call it—with all the colors of the spectrum in it. And he said, "The old bodies come and walk through this flowing color, and when they get on the other side, they are brand-new and beautiful."

There's something real about eternity. We cannot see it. We don't understand the half that's been told. But we sort of understand the half that *hasn't* been told. All I say is, "O Lord, I don't know where it is, what it is, or how it's going to be, but I love it—because You're Lord and I can trust You." Coming to this kind of trust in Him and His love wipes out forever all fear of the hereafter—and of the here and now—for ourselves and for our loved ones.

O my God, my life is cast down upon me [and I find the burden more than I can bear]; . . . Yet the Lord will command His loving-kindness in the daytime, and in the night His song shall be with me, a prayer to the God of my life.

(Psalm 42:6, 8 TAB)

5. Depression—And Joy!

It was pouring rain. I was thousands of miles from home, and I wanted to cry. Was it because it was Easter, or because it was raining, or because I was just plain lonely?

It was the first Easter I'd been separated from my kids. It's funny how many families are together on Easter, I mused. I'm realistic enough to know that there are problems in most homes, however neat and happy they look from the outside, and yet—

Outside my window, I could see husbands and wives and kids dressed up and headed for Easter services. Where did I fit? Certainly not with any of them. I'd feel like an intruder. And I didn't fit either with the young set in their careless approach to life, joyful as it seemed. It was part of my past, not to be resurrected.

Face it, Iverna. You don't fit. You're a misfit, and you feel it more strongly because it's a special day and the rest of the world is celebrating with all the excitement that accompanies a holiday.

But what is a misfit? Something placed where it doesn't fit, where it doesn't belong. But who placed me where I am? Am I a victim of circumstances, or is there a God who is the Lord of all circumstances?

Ten minutes of internal conversation and prayer led me to the conclusion that I was not a misfit, not really. By His placement, I was an exact fit. It was only by my unwarranted comparison of myself with others and their apparent lot in life that I didn't fit. But they wouldn't have fit the slot God designed for me, either.

This was the key, then, to my depression. I had stepped out of rank and coveted another place than the one He had designed for me. But I, and only I, am qualified and equipped to fill the place I'm in. With this awareness newly kindled within me, I regrouped myself, phoned the kids to wish them a Happy Easter, and went on my way to church, satisfied, knowing somehow that I was to be a blessing in a way that no one else in that church could be.

By God's grace, my depression was quickly dispelled, but for many people, depression is so long lasting it becomes a way of life.

The world is full of people who are depressed. No one is immune. And depression is very real, very dangerous, because it is so easy for the devil to move in on depression and cause us to destroy ourselves.

A few years ago, after an evening service, I met a sixteen-year-old girl who asked me for an appointment to discuss her family problems. We set a time for the following week, and I sent her away with the usual words of encouragement. Shortly after midnight, the local hospital phoned me to say a dying girl was calling my name. I hurried down and discovered our appointment was scheduled too late. In her depression, she had gone home and shot herself.

Depression is especially prevalent among singles who don't have enough to occupy their minds or their time, who don't have any particular goals they're working toward, who don't have anyone with whom to share their leisure hours, who are away from the place they call home. Loneliness triggers a lot of depression.

We're made so that our emotions begin to over-react and over-respond when it gets dark outside. Our intellect takes a recess after the sun goes down, and our heart takes over. Most of the loneliness that singles experience is worse after sunset. But you can do something about it.

Plan activities for the evening hours. Eat your evening meal later, at seven instead of at five. And set the table— linen, silver, flowers. Don't slop together just any old thing, but plan your meal so that it will be attractive to look at, interesting to eat, satisfying emotionally as well as nutrition-ally adequate. Look forward to it.

I have a friend who plays little games with herself, and I often do it, too. She will say to herself, "Tonight you can have a bubble bath." And she schedules a time for it, and looks forward to it; she doesn't just plain go in and take a bath to get clean or to relax her body. She plans it in her mind. She looks at the *TV Guide* and decides what she'll watch. And she thinks about how she's going to luxuriate in her bubble bath, really enjoying it. She stacks her favorite records on the record player and climbs in the tub— Ah-h, it's so soothing and rewarding. It really is. So wonderfully relaxing.

Of course, as soon as you've sunk down in the bubbles, the phone rings. It'll do it every time. But the plan is good. And even if the ring is on account of a wrong number, it helps dispel the loneliness, too.

There's something else you can do about loneliness. Do something new. Enlarge your life. Pick up a brochure at your local community college or technical school or city recreation department. Find out about the many activities going on in night groups—art classes, creative-writing classes, ceramics, flower arranging, all kinds of things. Fun things.

Once when I was pastoring, and I was just going, going, all the time, ministering to people, people, people, I felt I was headed for a breakdown. On the verge of depression, I couldn't stand all work and no play another week. Then one night I saw an announcement in the newspaper about an antiquing class being held at a time when I could be free. Without telling anyone, I went to the class, knowing no one there. I did not identify myself, did not say I was a minister. For six glorious weeks, I was known only as Iverna in a class where everybody was learning how to antique furniture. Nobody told me their troubles, nobody asked me for advice. I had a ball. It was exciting.

Find something you like to do, and do it. Just plain enjoy being you. If you'll work at being good company for yourself, you won't have to be lonesome.

Hobbies can be lifesavers. And hobbies do not take artistic abilities. Too many of us have had the attitude, "I can't have a hobby because I'm not talented."

Ridiculous! I'm an absolute klutz— When I used to have my children beside me in church, I drew pictures for them to keep them amused. And they'd whisper and say, "What is it?" They couldn't tell whether it was a tree or a dog. (It wasn't so embarrassing after they got old enough to read. I could draw a tree and write t-r-e-e under it. Then they knew.)

In recent years, even I have taken up a hobby. I learned

how to take a dumb little wire, string some beads on it, and twist it around to make earrings. You have no idea the sense of accomplishment I feel when I sit and waste two hours making three pair of earrings nobody will ever wear. But I am so proud of them. I say, "Oh, aren't they beautiful! I made them."

I don't want to hear about what little talent it took, because it took a lot of talent as far as I'm concerned. Everybody needs something that they can accomplish, something that results in a finished product. I'm going to keep on making earrings because I enjoy it. Maybe you like to write poetry—feel free. Or maybe working crossword puzzles is a great challenge to you. Go to it. Just be sure to do something that expresses yourself. And do enough of it that you don't have time to be lonely.

If your job isn't one that keeps you involved in interaction with other people, maybe you'll choose an off-duty activity that lets you express the social side of your nature. Be a Red Cross volunteer worker, a Gray Lady in the hospital, a school lunchroom volunteer, a political campaigner. People whose lives are put to good use sixteen hours a day seem to welcome instead of dread eight hours of solitude out of the twenty-four.

Because depression is so common, we need not only to understand it in ourselves and take steps to prevent occasions for it, but we need also to learn how to minister healing to others caught in its depths.

Peter was depressed. He said, "I give up. I'm not spiritual. I don't know what God wants. I don't know where Jesus is. I don't know anything, and nuts to all of it. I'm going fishing." And he just took off. Then the Lord showed up. "Hello, Peter. How are you?" And this is exactly what He's saying to us, and what we're saying to one another. "How are you?"

Sometimes people give us an honest answer. Instead of saying, "I'm fine, thanks, how are you?" they look straight at us and say, "I'm just awful. And getting worse. Man, I'm really down."

Don't take such a confession lightly. And don't add to their depression by saying, "You shouldn't feel that way. You have the Lord." If there's anything I don't want to hear when I'm depressed, that's it. And I don't want a long inventory of all I have that I should be thankful for. "Oh, look at you. How fortunate you are! Your children are serving God. And you have this great call of God on your life."

I know what I have. If I didn't know I had it, I'd be a moron. I already know what I have, and I'm still depressed. When you try to cheer me up, you don't help. You just incite me to anger or to deeper depression. If you're going to get involved with me at all, get involved with me with an understanding like my High Priest has. Be touched with feeling for my infirmity. Don't judge me for it, and don't give me 922 reasons why I shouldn't feel the way I do. Instead, say, "Iverna, I understand."

And if you understand and want to help, come and love me. Love covers a multitude of missing the mark. Depression is a missing the mark, a sin. It's less than what God wants for us. We haven't even gotten up to the target yet when we're depressed, but that doesn't make our depression any less real.

I said once, "Lord, what does it mean when it says we're to cover a multitude of sins?"

He said, *You're a Band-Aid.*

I said, "A Band-Aid?"

He said, *That's right. What do you do with a Band-Aid, Iverna?*

I said, "You put it on a sore."

He said, *How long does it stay there?*

I said, "Till it gets well."

He said, *Right on.*

You move in and cover that person with your caring, your prayers. "I'm with you, because I know what it's like. I want you to know I'm here. I'm praying, I'm believing God. Hallelujah! I'm excited with what God is doing in you."

I give myself to the depressed person. And I tell her about the time I thought I would die. The pastor was preaching against depression, and he was saying, "God never intended His people to be depressed," and he went on and on and on. If there was anyone the least bit depressed when they came into his church, they went out totally depressed. And those who were manic-depressive to start with— Wow! Someone had to dig them out of the sidewalk!

We need to understand that negative emotions are going to come. We're created that way. God wants our emotions to be healthy, to be God-directed and Christ-centered, and He is working on it. But in the meantime, there are some negative things that happen in our lives, and as we confront them, we learn what to do with them.

When you are depressed, you have not lost the Lord. You are not depressed because you have sinned. It isn't the dealings of God that cause you to be depressed. That is not His way. The Lord doesn't depress you, He corrects you. You don't browbeat your children. You don't just make them feel guilty. You help them to understand their guilt and give them a way out with a spanking.

Spanking has certain psychological relaxing results—you know at least it's over. You paid the price. You feel good. That's the way the Lord corrects us—He chastens us, but He doesn't make us feel depressed. That's something else. You're depressed because you're dying unto your self. It's something you're going through. Learn to accept it just like you learn to accept your premenstrual depression. You know you have it. You've had it for years and years, every month of your life. But you keep forgetting it.

"Oh, I don't know what's wrong with me. I feel so—"

Aren't we stupid? We have it every month twelve months a year for forty-odd years, but we forget to reckon with it. As we get a little older, finally it dawns on us. "Oh, I know what's wrong! It's *that time* in my cycle." And immediately we feel better because we know it's not going to last forever. There are spiritual cycles of life, just as there are physiological cycles. We are being changed from glory, to glory, to glory, to glory. He's changing us. On the way, we may go through some depressing things, but we are moving on out above them.

You get up in the morning, you're weary. The house is in a mess. What do you do? You clean the house. Of course you're weary, but you get on with it. You're going to have depression. You're going to have wars. You're going to have inner conflicts. Identify them, shift gears, and go on from there. Get on with the program.

Grow up in the Lord. When you begin to do this, exercising this control, ruling your own spirit, ruling your own life, you'll see more and more victory.

*Charm can be deceptive and beauty doesn't last,
but a woman who fears and reverences God shall be
greatly praised.*

(Ecclesiastes 31:30 TLB)

6. You and Men—

Suppose, for reasons that are nobody's business but our own, we choose not to marry. And we can do that without ever apologizing or explaining our whys to anybody. We are persons created separately and individually, and we have a right to say, "I choose to be single."

If we're honest in our choice, if this is what we really want, we are assuming, under God, the responsibility for our own life. Having chosen this walk, we must learn to be wise with our life. We have to discard all our excuses and seek to be fulfilled in every area where we can be fulfilled. And we won't be entitled to complain about the state we're in— because it's the one we have chosen.

One of the vital areas in which we need to recognize some principles, make some decisions, and live by them is in our relationships with the men in the world. They're there—you can't just ignore them or pretend they don't exist. How should you relate to them?

"But"—more than one single has told me, "I'm afraid of men." Sometimes it's a never-married who grew up without brothers, led a secluded life, and has never really known a male as a person. Sometimes divorcées or widows have husband scars that have made them withdraw protectively from all male companionship.

To overcome fear of men, stop generalizing. All men are no more alike than all women are. You may have to force yourself to engage in conversation with men for a while, but go ahead and do it. The rewards will be worth the effort. Learn to be interested in them as persons, and you'll soon discover that they're capable of reciprocating. You can't get over your fear of men by abstaining from fellowship with them. If you encounter a man who disappoints you or even insults you (and what insults one might be received as a gracious compliment by another), don't reinstate a whole set of defenses. Check him off as having a problem, and let it be his, not yours.

I grew up with four brothers, another man who lived with us in our home, and my dad. I know men. I'm used to conversing with them. And sometimes in my ministry to women, I get lonely just to talk to guys. They're different from us.

It's fine for me to find fellowship with a man, but I have to set the limits. I can't usurp—take from someone else what is their right.

There are lots of ways to find male companionship without threatening anyone. We can talk to male friends on the job, talk to our boss, to co-workers. The man at the bus stop. Your pastor. The postman. Just don't fall into the trap of trying to meet all of your needs for male companionship from one person. Take a little bit from a lot—and nobody will get hurt, nobody will get any funny ideas.

There is always somewhat of a caution in the heart of a married woman toward singles—unmarried women, widows, divorcées. Often the married woman considers us a threat, thinking, "She's after my husband!" Sometimes she's right.

Usually, however, we are only innocently after her husband's temporary attention. We're not trying to split a home, but sometimes, without even thinking it through, we exert a wrong kind of influence, disruptive of peace and harmony in the home. Maybe it's been such a long time since we've had a guy say, "Oh, you look so lovely," that we read into it more than he means, and we flutter our eyelashes and start to fall apart. And he doesn't show very good sense, either.

"What kind of perfume is that you're wearing?" he asks, inhaling deeply, with a sick grin on his face. When you tell him, he sniffs again and croons, "Lovely, lovely." Then he turns to his wife and says, "Honey, I wish you'd wear some—"

She glares at him, glares at you, and the evening is off to a rotten start.

It's always our responsibility in our relationships with others to set that home at ease, not to take more from that family than is ours, not to usurp anything. We don't have a right to go into the home of a married couple and capture the man's attention for an evening. If *he* doesn't know any better, *we* should. We have a responsibility to keep the wife happy, to let her remain unthreatened by our presence.

The same rules apply if you're a divorcée whose husband has remarried. When I'm around my ex-husband and his wife, I show much attention to her. When I telephone, I never ask for him. If one of the kids answers, I say, "Is either your mom or your dad there?" In the beginning, one would get on one line and one on the other. But they don't have to do that now—they know they can trust me. I'm not out to usurp what doesn't belong to me.

Married men can be your good friends. Let them, but keep it on a platonic basis. Don't give me any nonsense about, "We didn't know what was happening, and all of a sudden we discovered we were in love." You are the sensitive one with the greatest capacity to manipulate, so you have to set the limits—always. Your conversation should not be about his needs or yours. Enjoy a peer fellowship with one another on non-personal subjects—they're safer.

Women who work outside the home almost invariably find themselves encountering men on the job. Sometimes these relationships are happy ones, sometimes not. If a single feels that her male employer or co-worker is hostile toward her, she should take inventory of herself.

"What do I do to incite his anger? Have I played Miss Prude? Do I have that hungry look that keeps him on the defensive? Is there something in me that aggravates him?" And if you finish your inventory without turning up anything, pray, "Lord, help me. Reveal it to me."

There is always the possibility that your boss's hostility is a spiritual thing, if he is a godless man and Christ is in you. The Holy Spirit rises up against unholiness, and unholiness also rises up against holiness. This could account for his reactions.

Remember that Jesus loved everyone, and He loved them with a right kind of love. We can pray, "Lord, graft in me Your love, with which to show forth love to this person."

But don't be a rug, a doormat. If you honestly pray, and the Lord doesn't reveal something to you in yourself that needs correction, and the hostility persists, change jobs. You never can tell what good things God has in store for you somewhere else.

Don't marry your job. Don't worry so much about tenure, security, promotions, and such that you stay in a job that makes you miserable. But you have to hold on so you can retire when you hit sixty-five? Baloney! It's not worth it. You might not live that long. Get a job you enjoy—under a boss who appreciates you.

Even where singles are not regularly thrown with men in job situations, there seems to be in many of them a fear that men are lying in wait to take advantage of women without husbands in business affairs. The Scripture warns men against this, giving many "bewares" to those who take advantage of the widow. But we can't count on their reading the Scripture, we need to call upon God's wisdom for ourselves. If our prayer life is where it ought to be, we'll begin to see through things. Most often, when we are taken advantage of by someone, it's because we have been lazy in our own thinking, and have turned our affairs over to someone else when we should have done what was necessary to handle them ourselves.

When we permit someone else to do our thinking for us, we put ourselves in a position where we could be violated. And we almost deserve it. Don't be too lazy to think things through for yourself.

In Christian circles today, there is often a great deal of confusion about what a single woman's relationship to men—and to God—ought to be. In the midst of increased teaching emphasis on headship and authority and scriptural order in the home, the single woman naturally asks, "But who is my headship?" It's a good question, and a necessary one. To answer it, let's look first at one of the basic Scriptures dealing with headship.

Scripture says,

"But I would have you know that the head of every man is Christ; and the head of the woman is the man; and the head of Christ is

God. Every man praying or prophesying, having his head covered, dishonoureth his head. But every woman that prayeth or prophesieth with her head uncovered dishonoureth her head: for that is even all one as if she were shaven. For if the woman be not covered, let her also be shorn: but if it be a shame for a woman to be shorn or shaven, let her be covered. For a man indeed ought not to cover his head, forasmuch as he is the image and glory of God: but the woman is the glory of the man. For the man is not of the woman; but the woman of the man. Neither was the man created for the woman; but the woman was created for the man. For this cause ought the woman to have power on her head because of the angels. Nevertheless neither is the man without the woman, neither the woman without the man, in the Lord. For as the woman is of the man, even so is the man also by the woman; but all things of God. Judge in yourselves: is it comely that a woman pray unto God uncovered? Doth not even nature itself teach you, that, if a man have long hair, it is a shame to him? But if a woman have long hair, it is a glory to her: for her hair is given her for a covering. But if any man seem to be contentious, we have no such custom, neither the churches of God."

I Cor. 11:3–16

This Scripture has been a source of confusion to those who fail to realize that the New Testament is interested in teaching principles, ways of life, kingdom life. Instead of giving us a whole list of rules to guide us all through life, the Lord lays out kingdom principles.

If we know the principle of honesty, we don't need a Scripture that tells us in what areas we ought to be honest. We know to be honest in everything. If we know the principle of purity, we don't have to wonder in which specific areas we should be pure. We know the principle of purity means to be pure in everything.

In this Scripture dealing with the principle of headship, God is not dealing with long hair versus short hair. He is dealing with the principle that God is the head of Christ and responsible for Christ; Christ is the head of man and responsible for him; man is the head of woman and responsible for her.

One extreme teaching on headship concludes that women can never deal directly with the Lord, that women can get only indirectly, from the man, whatever God is saying.

The other extreme is for the woman to take the attitude, "I don't need a man. I don't need any covering. I'm just me by myself, and I speak absolutely right on through, straight to God." But Paul says that it's a shame for a woman to be uncovered. On the other hand, for a man to be covered would be a shame, because a covering says, in essence, "I'm not directly responsible to God. I'm directly responsible to someone else who is exerting an authority over me before God." For a man to be uncovered is saying, "Lord, whatever Thou saith unto me, I will stand and do—no matter what."

Now, this Scripture is speaking primarily to the married women, not to those without husbands. As a matter of fact, some translations read *wife, husband*, rather than *man, woman*. The implication is that women who say, "My husband doesn't really know the Lord, but I am really moving out to know God," are uncovering themselves. When the woman says, "My husband is my covering," she may even know more spiritually than he, she may be the one who says, "Now let's read the Bible, now let's pray, now let's go to church." But that doesn't change her covering if she's in right relationship in her home. If she is in right relationship, she is blessing her husband with the knowledge of the Lord, and he is blessing and covering her.

Why is this covering so important? Scripture says, "Because of the angels." There are two different interpretations of this. One is that the Scripture is speaking of evil angels, who lie in wait to make prey of women who are not under the covering of a man. The other interpretation is that it's speaking of God's angels who know the right order of headship, and are checking to see if we're living in the realm of right relationship. Paul says, "Let the women be submissive. Let them understand their rightful place."

Headship is a term referring to authority, not superiority. It is positional, not qualitive. It doesn't mean that we're less than man, inferior to him. A lot of women today are angry about the curse that came upon them when Eve fell and caused Adam to sin. The Lord said, "For this, you are going to be made subject to your husband." That's a fact, whether we like it or not. It is the Word of God. We have been put in a position subordinate to man.

The Lord said, "I created man for Me. I wanted fellowship. Then I created woman to bless man, but instead of blessing man, she got out of order." She didn't confer with Adam when the serpent came and suggested it would be all right for her to do something God had forbidden. She made the decision by herself and partook of the forbidden fruit. Then she said to Adam, "I've already done it. You might as well join me."

And the Lord said, "All right, Eve, because you took the lead in the wrong way, I'm going to give him a stab at it. You're going to be subjected to the man." And it has been that way ever since.

Submission is not action, submission is attitude, and you don't have to be in a marriage relationship to learn submission. God provides many opportunities for us to come under protective headship. Everyone must learn submission, and if you do not learn it in one area, you will learn it in another.

If a man doesn't learn submission under God, the Lord puts him in a vise on his job. The Lord will let the situation get more and more intolerable because he *is* going to learn to submit. The same thing is true for women. I did not learn submission in the bonds of matrimony, but I have since learned, and am learning, submission in every area of my life. The Lord has placed me in situations where I am forced to submit constantly. Now, instead of submitting to one man, I say to every pastor in every church where I go to minister, "You are my headship for this week as far as ministering goes. I'm in your church. I'll be obedient to minister whatever you want me to minister, and to refrain from doing what you tell me not to do. And if I say anything wrong, if I preach the wrong doctrine, or if I hurt you in any way, I want you to correct me." I need his covering. I need that protection.

I am fortunate because my brother Judson has assumed a position of spiritual authority over me, and he reaffirms it every year. He says, "Iverna, I'll be your spiritual headship. Anytime anyone wants to know anything about your walk or your ministry, have them call me. Anytime you have a question, anytime you need prayer, call me."

First Peter 5:5 states: "Likewise, ye younger, submit yourselves unto the elder. Yea, all of you be subject one to another, and be clothed with humility: for God resisteth the proud, and giveth grace to the humble." How important it is for us to get the chips off of our shoulders, to learn to submit to others, men *or* women.

Just as I submit to other pastors in my ministry, so during your eight-hour-a-day job, you are to submit to your immediate authority.

If God is Lord of all, He's Lord over my headship, too. He's Lord over the pastors who are delighted I've come, and

He's Lord over the pastors who have me because somebody pressured them into it.

I can submit to every one of them because I am, through this submission, submitting to the Lord. They can't hurt me unless the Lord lets them. I know that, and He knows I know it. That's how we can afford to submit ourselves to other people.

Sometimes people tell me, "Oh, Iverna, you give too much to this group or this person." It's never true, because they have to give an account to their superiors, who have to give an account to their superiors, who have to give an account— Ultimately, account is given to the Lord. And because I have submitted myself to others as unto Him, He's taking care of me through it all.

If we don't come into proper submission in our relationships, we are wide open to deception. At the basis of many false cults was a woman out from under authority who got a kooky idea from some source and refused correction from men, leading some of them astray. In demonology, in spiritualism, there are far more women witches and mediums than male warlocks and mediums.

We need to be grateful to God that we're not involved in deception. We need to thank the Lord that we have not been deceived. I *want* to be submissive. I *want* to be subjected. I *want* to be in my rightful place in the Lord so that I'm covered and protected and I won't go astray down a wrong path believing I'm doing the right thing. The Lord has set every provision for us whereby we can be totally protected if we will submit ourselves.

Submission doesn't make me feel inferior—it almost makes me feel stronger. And I'm not a candidate for women's lib, although it has some good points. If a woman is doing the same job that a man is doing, she ought to get the same pay. We all agree that makes sense.

But I don't like the unisex idea. I don't want to be equal with man in the sense of sameness with him. I don't want to be treated like a man. There's something special to me about walking to a door and knowing he's going to open it for me. I love it.

Recently a doctor said to me, "I do not agree with you. I think your position is antiquated. I think you're way back—"

"Oh, my position is much older than you have any idea," I told him. "It's about six thousand years old."

The women's lib movement has stirred up rebellion in the hearts of women everywhere, rebellion we didn't even know existed. It was all buried and hidden, and nobody had a problem with it—except the Lord. He said, *I see something in you that's not right, and I'm coming for a Church without spot or wrinkle, one that's been perfected by Myself. I'll have to squeeze out that dirty core of rebellion, that you might be healed.* The women's liberation movement is permitted of God, that the rebellion might surface, be recognized, and be healed.

7. You and Sex—

Sex. What's *it* like out there in No Man's Land?

No, married people don't usually come right out and ask you point-blank, most of them. They're too polite for that. But we can read the question in their curious glances, in their occasional lifted eyebrows, in their outright stares that are eloquent with wondering. "How do you suppose she handles it?" "Does she have a boyfriend on the side?" "A too close girl friend?" "Or is she the do-it-yourself type?"

Chances are, most of the married people who look the question at you, honestly wonder how *they'd* handle it if they were suddenly bereft of their mates. There's no argument about it, our sexuality is an important part of us.

God has given us a sexual appetite, and He says that in the bonds of marriage we can satisfy this appetite, and outside of the bonds of marriage, we may not.

What then are we singles supposed to do with our sexual drives?

We have many appetites of the flesh. Appetites are not sins; they are not lustings. Lust is an appetite that's improperly accentuated. If we've just eaten a more than adequate meal, and we're still craving more, we're lusting. But if we haven't eaten all day, and we feel hungry, that's appetite.

Like it or not, we are capable of living with an unsated area or areas in our appetites. There are some appetites we singles are permitted to satisfy: We may eat to satisfy our appetite for food. We may read to satisfy our appetite for knowledge. We may satisfy our appetite for physical affection by a hug or friendly pat from our children or a friend. There are other appetites which we may legitimately satisfy, but for the unmarried woman, sex is not one of them. That has to remain an unsated area for us, in which we have to continually guard ourselves against temptation.

It's amazing how free from temptation one can feel when it's been only a theoretical thing for a while, when it hasn't actually knocked on your door for a season.

Not long ago, I experienced something which shocked me back into the realization of my own vulnerability in this area—and gave me a new appreciation of the power of God in helping us withstand temptation.

I was away from home in a strange city, eating dinner in a restaurant and casually watching people come and go. When I saw a well-dressed man approaching my table, I looked up at him to see what he wanted. He smiled and introduced himself and showed such an apparently genuine interest in me that I was soon chatting about myself and my family, never suspecting that he was a wolf in sheep's clothing. I was even bold enough to admit to him that I was a minister.

The man accepted with friendly approval everything I had to say, and as we drank our coffee together, I felt warm and cared for—and was completely disarmed and totally unprepared for the proposition that followed. But what startled me more than the proposition was my honest internal response to it. I wanted to accept!

As I forced the right words of rejection to be spoken, I prayed he wouldn't see through them and discover the longing I felt within, the longing to be loved, the longing to be "special" to somebody.

When he left my table and began to search for a new prospect for his amorosity, my emotional involvement ended, and I could breathe and think clearly again. The experience taught me that we are never, of ourselves, immune to temptation. But the Lord delivers us from temptation as we pray that He will. As the Scripture promises, He "will with the temptation make a way to escape." Our part is to call upon Him and to be obedient to do what we know to do. If we entertain the temptation, and try to rationalize our way to succumb to it, we take ourselves out from under His protection.

Overcoming temptation in the sexual area may be particularly difficult for young widows whose husbands were suddenly snatched away by death. Their sexual appetite was accustomed to being satisfied regularly within the bonds of matrimony. It was a vital part of their relationship to one another. The blessing and peace of God was upon it. Then, all at once—nothing. It is especially important for young widows to safeguard themselves by avoiding occasions for temptation. It is important for the rest of us without husbands, too.

For all of us, there are certain times in our monthly cycle when we're more prone to thoughts of sexual activity than at other times. At such times, we need to take the precaution of shielding ourselves from known stimulation. Don't watch sexy TV programs. Don't read romantic novels. Don't go to see some mushy love movie. There are better things for us to do when we're weak. We shouldn't torture ourselves by unnecessary exposure to difficult situations.

It's better to divert our attention—go bowling, run around the block, play tennis, visit a friend, take in a museum or the zoo. Do something else. Think about something else.

I find there are times when I don't like to be around couples. It just plain bothers me when my cravings are deep. What's bugging me isn't necessarily a specifically sexual hunger. Maybe it's just a need to be part of my own couple, to belong totally to somebody. At such times, as gracefully as I can, I get away from situations that are not easy for me. I protect myself from frustration and temptation.

We all know that premarital sex is wrong, that extramarital sex is wrong, because the Bible is so plain about it. Fornicators and adulterers have no reservations in heaven. But why? Is this just an arbitrary rule that God invented to plague us? Or is it a reflection of something basic to our natures, basic to the act of sexual union itself? Let's take a look at it.

The Word says, speaking of marriage, "And they shall be one flesh" (Gen. 2:24). The expression doesn't refer only to sexual intercourse, but intercourse is part of what's involved. There is a bond of permanency that comes from sexual union, and it is usually far more significant to the female than to the male. When you've engaged in sexual activity with a man, you feel like *his*—a part of him—and you feel that he's a part of you. And when he rises from your intimate bed and goes home, whether to his wife, his dormitory room, or to his bachelor apartment, part of you goes with him. Something is missing from you. You're no longer a whole person, you're part of one, a fractional leftover.

When God outlawed sex outside of marriage, outside the bond of permanency, He did it in recognition of the nature He had already planted in us. And from the many fallen women I've counseled, I've learned that the awful trauma of guilt resulting from illicit sexual activity was minor compared to the sense of loneliness and hollowness and wantonness that were left when the illicit lover was gone.

Oh, yes, I've heard some, during their little "affairs," say, "Oh, this is being such a meaningful experience for me." But afterward, the meaning changed, and they paid a horrendous price. There was an aching emptiness left in them that no other person could ever fill.

Before my own marriage went on the rocks, I used to look at my husband in a group to try to see whether I thought he was handsome or not. But try as I might, I couldn't see him objectively. I could see the men in the group, and I could see my husband, but I couldn't see him separately as *one* of the men in the group. We *were* one flesh. My whole life was united with his.

Today my ex is married to another woman, and has been married to her for ten years. I *still* can't see him as one of the men in a group, because he was once a part of me. It's a statement of fact when God says, *Listen. When you come together, it's marriage. It's a bond of permanency. The two of you shall be one flesh.*

If you've already engaged in premarital sex or other extramarital sexual activity, confess it, forsake it, and ask God to forgive you. Ask Him to heal your brokenness, to impart to you wholeness, to let you begin a new life. He is the remedy for all our mistakes. And He lets us start all over again without them—as if they'd never happened.

But if you haven't already succumbed to the temptation to

go to bed with someone not your husband, praise God, and don't be tempted to add a scar to your life. Begin to learn what joy there is in thinking on the things that are pleasant and virtuous and of good report. Think of all the things that are of the Lord, and let victory come into your life—even in this.

What about masturbation as a means of satisfying your sexual appetite when you have no husband? That's a big question in many circles because of the extreme teaching that we used to hear—if you masturbated, you would go crazy, lose your mind, break out in some horrid pimple disease, and go straight to hell. None of this was true, but people believed it, and so sometimes, it seemed to happen. Then some insights came into the world in social work, and the teaching became almost the opposite— Anything goes. Satan's lies became rampant—"Your sex desire will die if you don't yield to it." "The more the merrier."

What's the truth about masturbation? Does the Bible have anything to say about it? No, not directly. The Bible says clearly, "Flee fornication, and do not commit adultery," but it never mentions masturbation specifically. You won't find the word in any list of dos or don'ts in the Bible.

That's not surprising. The Bible doesn't say anything specific about a lot of things that are wrong. It doesn't have to. God says He's written His law on our hearts, and if a thing is wrong for us, we'll know it. We won't need a list from anybody.

It's time for us to mature to the principles taught in the Bible, to grow up a little bit.

The Scripture is absolute about some things: You absolutely must confess your sins, you absolutely must receive

Christ as your Savior. You have to come through Jesus if you're going to know God. You're to obey the great commandment to love God with all your heart and mind and soul and to love your neighbor as yourself. But in many other areas, the Scriptures don't deal with absolutes but with attitudes—the motives, the whys of life.

God looks on the heart, and He would have us examine our hearts for ourselves:

Why do you want to do these things? Why do you encourage your mind to dwell on sensual pleasures, bringing you into shady actions you're ashamed of? Why don't you choose to concentrate on what is lovely, and of good report? When we begin to see the true answers to these questions we'll have come a long way toward deliverance.

Jesus didn't come with a list of dos and don'ts so He could condemn us. He said, "I am come that you might have life more abundantly. I'm come to bring you everything that you lack in your life. I'm come to help you to victory. I'm the way, the truth, the life. I'm everything you'll ever need. I love you, and you can rest in My love."

That doesn't mean that God is going to take away the sexual appetite He created in you. It's going to be there—and you *don't* have to feed it to keep it alive. There *are* times when it will be a pain or a problem to you. Masturbation can relieve sexual tension, but as in the satisfying of other appetites, the relief is only temporary. The tension will build up again, the appetite will return. And afterward, if you've got more guilt than you had tension to begin with, you've lost the whole ball game, and started on a vicious circle. Self-indulgence and guilt might prove a greater problem to you than self-denial and tension.

Specifically sexual gratification isn't the only outlet, the only release, for sexual energy. Much of it can be channeled into non-sexual creative activity—playing the piano, mowing the lawn, excelling in competitive sports. A man goes off to war, and right away his wife paints the house, makes new draperies, enrolls in a course in European history and makes the dean's list. Paul poured out his creative life energy in spreading the Gospel. And he said, "When I am weak, then am I strong. His strength is made perfect in my weakness."

We can apply that in our own lives, to the glory of God, and we can know that we will not be tested beyond what we can bear. There has no temptation taken us but such as is common in man. We're not the only ones going through it. There are thousands of people who are separated from their mates by reason of sickness, or jobs, or armed services—all of these things—who are still faithful, who aren't masturbating, who aren't sleeping with someone who isn't their marriage partner. And if the world can, how much more can you who know His strength? It's a subtle trick of the devil to come into your mind and make you think you can't live without having your sexual appetites satisfied with sexual activity. The devil is a liar.

So many people have the erroneous idea that if I want something, I ought to have it. But that's not true. We teach our kids differently. They see something, and they say, "I want it," and we say, "Your wants won't hurt you. You can't have it. You're not going to get it." If it's good for our kids not to have everything they want, it's good for us to learn to exert that kind of control over ourselves, too.

Do we want? Let's not lie about it. There are times when we want very much. There's just no way in No Man's Land, that's all. Are you going to die? No. Wish you would? Sometimes.

Christians should be aware that extreme involvement with satisfying oneself with erotic love—in marriage or out of it—very nearly borders on hedonism. It is sensual worship. Licentiousness. And the Bible doesn't recommend it. Neither does your own conscience.

If you've started down a wrong path, based on an attitude that says, "I have this drive, and I'm going to please me," you're on a dangerous route. You need to pray, "Lord, am I functioning in an excessive manner in wanting to please myself with sensual passion? Am I exhibiting inordinate, lustful affection for myself? Help me, I pray, to replace this method of Satan with something pleasing to You. Help me establish a new habit pattern, Lord—I have such a tremendous need. I confess that something within me is driving me to lust. Please cleanse me, Lord. I don't want anything in my life that makes me ashamed before You. I don't want to open the door for Satan. Give me the help I need—let me glorify You with my body. Let me respect it as the temple of Your Holy Spirit."

This is an area where you've got to come to some understanding, some decision in yourself, and having done all, to stand, not caring who calls you a prude.

Sing praises to the Lord! Raise your voice in song to him who rides upon the clouds! Jehovah is his name—oh, rejoice in his presence. He is a father to the fatherless; he gives justice to the widows, for he is holy.

(Psalm 68:4–5 TLB)

8. You and Your Kids—

After I began to dwell in No Man's Land, I had to acknowledge a new role for God in caring for my children.

One day I was in Honolulu for a speaking engagement when I got a phone call from my daughter.

"Mom," she said, "I don't want to upset you, but I thought you ought to know that Dan called. He is very unhappy in school and wants to come home. I told him he could come for the weekend, because I could take care of him, and you would be home on Tuesday." I thanked her for the information and hung up the phone. Dan was fifteen. It was his first year away from home in boarding school.

I wish my first response had been to praise the Lord, but it wasn't. I was utterly disgusted. My vocal reaction was, "Great, Lord, that's just great. Here I am, over here doing Your work, clear across the ocean— How do You expect me to—" My grumble began to grow toward a crescendo, when He interrupted me, ever so gently.

Iverna, are we going to go this route again?

"Sorry about that," I said, and calmed down a little. But I wasn't exactly praising anybody yet.

Iverna, He went on, still all love and gentleness, *why don't you practice what you preach?*

I swallowed hard, went out on the little balcony opening off my room, and began to be obedient.

"Lord," I said. "I thank You for this marvelous opportunity to be an overcomer. Your Word says You will be a father to my children, and I've claimed this promise through all my years of raising them. And now I'm just saying, 'You're Dan's Father. Please say something to him.' "

After I had said "Amen" and "Hallelujah" a few times to try to bolster my courage, I went inside to get ready for the meeting. There's nothing like feeling totally defeated when you are scheduled to bring forth victory from your innermost being. So I was still praising the Lord for *my* sake when the phone rang again. It was Debbie.

"Mom, guess what? Dan just called me back, and he said that while he was in his room, the Lord spoke to him and said, 'Dan, your problem is that you're putting girls before Me.' " Wow!

Now, my children are not superspiritual kids. They're very normal, average American kids. I was thrilled, of course, that Dan could recognize his problem and make the necessary adjustments without wrecking his school situation. But I was twice thrilled to see the maturity that the Lord was bringing into his life. It was a sovereign work of God, not dependent on having mom there for a one-hour lecture.

I had prayed, "Lord, You're his Father. Say something to him." And the Lord had said something. Exactly what was needed.

Ideally, in God's perfect plan, the carrying out of parental responsibility is a two-person job—for a mother and a father. But when there isn't a father on the premises, you, the mother, have to do it by yourself. And you are able. With God's help.

It's well to begin with a prayer—"Lord, I gave birth to this child, but I will not hold it so tightly that You cannot move. It's Your child, and I'm Your child, so give me wisdom. God, help me to establish in this child the things that matter, the things that are important.

"Don't let me try to relive my childhood through him. Give me wisdom to see that I can't make up for my mistakes by perfecting my children. They belong to You. Lord, that's Your boy. Lord, that's Your girl. When things get difficult, give me grace to hear and obey Your voice without trying to seize control for myself."

When we have prayed aright, we can trust God to tell us what to do and to empower us to do it.

Don't think you have to chase all over the country to try to live near an uncle or a brother or a grandfather so your boys will have a good masculine image to copy, your girls a good male image to look up to. It's not necessary. There are good masculine images in your church, among Boy Scout leaders, school teachers, neighbors. And by your attitude—recognizing that boys get dirty, play rough, climb trees, and keep frogs in their pockets—you can help your son to grow up all boy and not sissy.

God's word promises that if we will train up a child in the way he should go, when he is old, he will not depart from it (Prov. 22:6).

"Train" does not mean to say a lot of words, or merely to see that your child gets to Sunday school.

The word train is a very strong word which in the Hebrew

means to actively engage in the participation of. I could read a lot of books on how to ski, how to stand on those two sticks, how to land a certain way, how to turn and jump, how to balance. I could memorize all of the theory. But until I started to practice, I couldn't know how to ski.

In the same way, it isn't by our much talking that we nurture or train up children. We have to be actively engaged in training them, in showing them what to do, how to act. And one of the most vital things in their training has to do with providing the atmosphere for a growing relationship with God. The old thing we've all heard so much—not forcing a child to go to church because when he gets older, he's going to resent it—is garbage. If you think you've got trouble with kids rebelling about going to church, release them from attendance and see what happens. They'll be ten times worse. If anything's going to happen to them in the Lord, it's going to happen in His presence, and He dwells in the praises of His people. Your church should be a place where the praise of God is abundantly evident.

When I reached my early teens, if I hadn't been forced to go to church, I would not have gone to church. But it wasn't up to me.

Dad said, "You're going to church."

"Okay," I said, "I'll go." And then, determined in my inner rebellion not to let churchgoing affect my life, I promised myself, "He can lead a horse to water, but he can't make me drink. They'll never get to me." Nevertheless, I was constantly in the presence of the Lord, and regardless of my inner resolves, there was something about the presence of the Lord— From time to time, He got through to me. It never would have happened if I hadn't been inside the church.

By faith in God, I have actively, to the best of my ability, involved my two kids in a prayer life. I didn't bring them in and sit them down in the living room and say, "Now, we're going to read the Word." I know some homes do this, some pastors teach it. But for us, it wouldn't have worked. Instead of taking a specific time to think spiritually, we talked with the Lord just any old time, and we said, "Praise the Lord" for all the good things, always. We acknowledged that God was in control of our lives.

It wasn't a superspiritual thing. We just handled things as they came along. We talked about pleasing the Lord, about how the Lord provided for us. Our talk of the Lord was a part of our daily lives. It never occurred to the kids not to say, "Oh, isn't the Lord good to us!" when we had an especially good Christmas. They knew that everything we received was from the Lord.

Recently, I was considering an opportunity to go to Rome. Talking to my son on the phone, I said, "Boy, I sure would love to take you to Rome with me if I go."

"Gee, I think that would really be neat!" he said.

"Okay, let's begin to pray the money in," I told him, and he agreed. That wasn't strange to Dan. We've lived that way. He's indwelt by the awareness that God has provided very well for us. He has experienced how good it is to trust Him for everything.

For all but two years of my own life, I've walked with the Lord. During those two years when I was backslidden, it was so hard *not* to think of Him, I had to work at it.

I'd be at a party, and somebody would use the Lord's name in vain. "Don't say that," I'd hear myself saying.

"What's the matter with her?" they'd wonder. Or somebody else would be sitting playing poker, and they'd begin to tell a sad story.

"What you need is Jesus," I'd say.

"Jesus?" they'd ask, looking at me as if I'd lost all my marbles. I couldn't depart from that faith.

I married while I was backslidden, and when I found myself expecting a child, I realized that I could not raise it without the help of the Lord, and so I decided to walk back to God.

It was tough coming back to Him. I got down and I said, "Lord, I'm ready to come back." I expected that when I walked in, the whole church would fall on their faces in a great victorious shout. They did—but I didn't feel a thing. It was as if the Lord said, *This kid has a little bit to learn. Because I love her so much, I'll have to see that she learns it.*

I had three months of nothing—no emotions, no feeling, no response, not anything. One day I was driving my car, working at my job as a traveling salesman, and I said, "Lord, if I never feel You again, if I never sense Your presence again, I'm still coming to spend eternity with You because Your word says You have to take me." At that point something broke inside me, and I had to pull my car off the road and worship the Lord.

I had been trained in the ways of God. I knew God, I really knew Him. I didn't just go to Sunday school—He was really a part of my life. And because of that, when I was old, I couldn't depart from the faith. I had departed from the action of it, temporarily, but I was still His kid out there. The Lord said, *See here. That's My wayward child. We're working on her.* And He still is.

If you are an absentee parent, and see your children only on weekends, the kindest and the highest training that you can do for them is to accept them and love them. You can't do a whole lot of instructing, because it will all get watered down or contradicted the minute they are back home, and they'll be confused, worse off than before. When you have them for a long summer, however, you can really get them into the Word, into church, and if you do it the right way, they can come to know the Lord, and be a powerful witness for good when they go back home.

Discipline is vital for a child's well-being and happiness as well as for your own survival. When Dr. Spock appeared on nationwide TV and renounced all of his advice that we shouldn't discipline our children, I got a little mad at him. We'd tried his theories, and they didn't work. Now what were we supposed to do, start over? As mad as I got at him, I got madder at us, because our instructions have been perfectly clear in the Word of God all along. "He that spareth his rod hateth his son: but he that loveth him chasteneth him betimes" (Prov. 13:24).

It's a trick of the enemy to frighten us about raising children today. It isn't any tougher to raise children today than it was to raise them in my day. It just seems like it.

And you *are* equipped to handle them. God's Word wouldn't tell you to train up a child in the way he should go if it was impossible for you to do it. Therefore, you don't have to fear. You can train and correct them.

What should you do about a teenager who is already out from under your authority? You've blown it somewhere, and they've taken control, and are living a life you don't approve. I learned what to do when that happened in my own family.

When I was preparing to leave Eugene, Oregon, to go to Phoenix, my daughter thought she wanted to become a nurse, and so, in September, I put her in a nurses' training school in Portland.

After I left the area, Debbie decided she didn't want to be a nurse. We were together for Thanksgiving, and she said, "I hate it all." But I encouraged her—insistently—to stick with it a little while, to finish out the year, and then we'd take another look at it.

As time went on, her letters got further and further apart, and my spirit was eating at me inside. I knew something was wrong, but I didn't know what it was. Finally, one day, I tried to phone her at school, but she wasn't there. No one could tell me where to locate her. I tried for two days, and when I finally reached her, she said, "Mother, you're going to be very upset with me, but I've quit school, and I've got a job. I've found a room, and I'm moving out today."

Debbie was nineteen years old. Legally, she had every right to do as she pleased. But she wasn't brought up that way. I was dying inside, and I knew that I had to be very wise. But before I could open my mouth to say anything, she let me have the real shocker.

"I have this boyfriend," she said. "He and I are looking at one another, but we don't know what we're going to do yet." I thought I'd die.

I hung up the phone and cried a little bit, and then I went to prayer and really got ahold of God. I couldn't find any release, any feeling that I should let her go, let her fly, let her mess up her life. Instead, I sensed that she was flying blind, out of control, and that God was holding me responsible for straightening her out. I called her back and said, "I want you home in twenty-four hours."

Debbie had never sassed me or anything like that in all of her life, but she said, "Mother! I'm nineteen years old! I already have a job, and I have a room, and this *is* what I'm going to do."

"Oh no, you're not, young lady," I said, with all the authority of a four-star general.

"You get yourself home. Bag and baggage." Then I hung up before she could argue about it. There was no legal way I could force her to do what I wanted. She knew it, and I knew it. God knew it too—I was counting on Him to see that she did the right thing.

I sat up till after midnight, looking out the window, praying, holding my breath, waiting. About one o'clock in the morning, I heard a car drive up. Debbie came in—very rigid, very angry, all her stuff in the car, very much on the defensive. Her attitude bristled with, "Okay, you got me. Now what?"

I'd never seen her like this in all her life. She'd never been a rebellious kid, but she was then. And she seemed determined to stay that way. Although she was a top-notch secretary, could type 100 words a minute, she took a job as a carhop! Every night one or more creepy males—long hair, hot cars, and blue jeans with patches—would slouch up to the front door and lean on the doorbell. When I opened the door, they'd say, "Debbie here?"

I'd call up, "Jesus, help me." And I'd say to them, "Debbie who?"

I was dying inside. This was so anti anything I had ever experienced in my home that I didn't know how to handle it. "O God, help me to know," I prayed. And when He had answered my prayer, I went to Debbie and spoke my piece.

"I don't care how much money you make, or how much money you pay me. When you're in my home, young lady, you will abide by my standards. From now on, you will be in every night by midnight."

"But mother," she wailed, "I'm almost twenty years old!"

"I don't care if you're forty," I insisted. "You're going to come in on time. And anytime you're going to be late, I want a phone call."

That marked the beginning of getting her back. Whenever she wasn't in on time, I was at the door to be introduced to whoever was with her.

I made her go to church, too. She hated it, but we went. Was it hard? Of course it was hard. Did I feel silly? Certainly. I felt absolutely idiotic. But something—or Someone—said, *It's got to be done and it's got to be done now or you're going to lose her.*

When it came time for me to move and go into the ministry again, I said, "I'm going, Debbie. You're old enough to make your own decisions. You may stay here if you like. But I'm going to tell you something. I'm afraid for you to stay here, because you've been under my canopy of faith, my headship and my covering, and if you remain here and I go there, you're going to have to become an individual on your own. The way you're running around with all these guys who are not walking with the Lord, and the way you're not yielded to the Lord at this time in your own life, scares me. But I won't force you this time."

I'd forced her back once, made her take another look at the situation, brought her under authority, and said, "Now you're a big girl and I will not force you. You do as you feel led to do." And then I prayed like crazy. It was touch and go for a few days.

One day she had a better job offer and she was staying, and the next day she found a roommate and she was staying. And the next day, she thought she might as well go with me. It was up and down, up and down, and I kept praying for dear life.

At almost the last minute, she packed up and went with Dan and me and began to submit herself to the Lord anew and afresh.

One night as she knelt at the altar of the church where God had led us, I leaned over and put my arm around her. "Lord Jesus," I prayed, "I thank You for bringing my daughter back to You, and I give her to You in the ministry. Lord, let both of our lives minister for You."

At that moment, all the stubborn rebellion broke in her, and she began to speak in tongues under a new anointing of the Holy Spirit. Within a year, she was married to a precious guy—and they were both called to the ministry!

There is no pat answer for raising kids, but there is a pat Lord. He is always there, and He will give you wisdom if you ask for it. He will even redeem your apparent unwisdom. He's done that for me a million times.

One time when Dan was going through a stubborn streak, I went to the door of his room, handled it just enough to loosen it, and then I kicked it open. His eyes about popped out of his head, and I leaned over, laid my hands on his back and said, "In the name of Jesus, I command this to leave." I promise you that if God hadn't redeemed that, Dan would hate God today.

The Lord will give you wisdom. Honestly, He will. He'll give you direction. Most of you have already read too many books on child rearing. Close them. Come back to *the* Book and say, "Lord, I cement myself to You, and I trust in You."

I never used to take this arbitrary a stand. But I do now, because that which is godless is getting written up in books more and more—"Just let them go and have their own way, let them do their own thing, don't cause rebellion in your child by forcing him." What's wrong with most kids is that they've had to survive too much permissiveness.

In a recent study, some psychologists discovered that women who were especially responsive to their husbands were the daughters, almost invariably, of very demanding fathers. Demanding discipline tends to produce successful kids. Permissiveness encourages low standards and ultimately engenders failure.

How will *they* ever learn to control themselves if we don't learn to refrain from things we want to do—and do the things that we don't want to do? I don't give in to every whim and every desire I have. By the grace of God, I've learned self-control, and that's why I can say to my kids, "You control your life."

Learn to control your own emotions, and it will be easy to teach your kids to control theirs. Learn to be submissive in the right areas, and you'll be able to teach submission to your children. As a man thinketh, so is he—and we can't very well impart to our children something we lack in ourselves.

Whenever you begin to question your ability to be a good parent to your child, remind yourself that the Lord never entrusts a child to an individual without first placing in that individual the ability to rear that child. Many people fall short in motherhood, but that isn't because they couldn't mother. It's because they wouldn't. When I was working in probation, I concluded that a child's natural mother is usually the best mother for that child. I've seen kids come out of lousy homes and be placed in ideal foster care and there become very unhappy children.

You don't have to be a psychologist to be a good mother. You just have to love. Love conquers.

The Bible goes so far as to suggest that loving one's

children isn't an innate thing. Genuine love has to be learned because it's quite different from our natural sentimentality and selfish affection.

I have met some women who very honestly have said, "I really don't think I love my child, because of a lot of things in his life."

I say, "Okay, let's learn to love that child," because the Word says that the older women should teach the younger women to love their children. You can learn to love. You can teach love—by influence and example.

If you really love your children, you'll do all you can to bring them up to be happy, well-adjusted members of society. Here, especially for the woman without a husband, the attitudes you communicate are of vital importance. By projecting a wrong attitude toward your ex-husband, you can teach your children that their absentee father is no good. You can project such an air of condemnation that you create self-hate in your son because he's male. And if you're raising a girl, you're setting her up for problems of acceptance, hurting her potential to be a successful wife. To counteract this very natural tendency in myself as a divorcée, God has enabled me to hold my ex-husband up to our children as a good father image. The only flaws they've seen in his life are ones they've discovered for themselves.

Kids need security, and we can give them that by our attitude, no matter what the circumstances are. We can reflect to them, "Hey, we are secure. I know where I'm going. I know what we're doing."

When they raise their eyebrows at you and say, "Oh, but you don't have daddy, and we don't have daddy," or when they ask, "Do you still love daddy?" you can hug them up and say, "Oh, isn't God good to us! Daddy loves you, and mother loves you." They'll buy it if you really mean it, if your heart is right, and they won't feel hollow inside.

When they come back from a visit with their father, don't start pumping them. "What did you do? What's daddy doing? What did he say? Did he talk about me? What does his wife do? Do you like her? Did daddy say anything about money? Did you remember to tell him you have a hole in your shoe?" Instead of turmoil, give them security.

If they have only one good outfit, put that outfit on them when your ex is going to pick them up. Make sure they're clean and sweet and look their very best. Say, "I'm so glad you could spend some time with your dad today. Have a ball, will you." After they're out of earshot, you can cry your eyes out. "Lord, cover them. Don't let them hear anything they shouldn't. Don't let them see anything wrong." But the kids don't know that. You give them security and confidence. You don't have to tell them lies. You just don't tell them everything.

What do you say to your kids about your ex-husband's girl friend when they say, "Do you like so and so?"

I say, "I'm so pleased that so and so is bringing happiness to daddy." There are ways. Start over. We have to grow up and be the mature ones if we don't want our children to suffer.

One time I was very money conscious, and inadvertently, without realizing it, I had been talking about everything in dollars and cents. Somebody would say, "Iverna, that's a pretty outfit."

"It oughta be," I'd say. "It cost enough—a whole lot more than I could afford."

It hit home to me that I had gotten into the habit of talking poverty when I heard my daughter say to my son one day,

"Mother doesn't have any money." The worry in her voice just killed me.

"Oh forgive me, Lord," I moaned. Then I went in to where Debbie was and asked her, "What did you say?"

She didn't bother to repeat it. She knew I had heard her, so she simply shrugged her shoulders and said, "Well, mother, it's true. You said you didn't have any money."

I laughed, trying not to sound fake. "Oh, what I meant was that I don't have any money right here in my purse. I've got money in the bank." I didn't lie. I *did* have money in the bank—a whole dollar—to keep the account open. But I made it sound like a million. And they believed me.

I learned something from that little conversation. Since then, I've done everything I can to help my children feel secure, no matter what my own needs have been.

Have I had my nights of crying my eyes out? Of course. I know what it is to tuck the kids in with joy, praise, and victory, and then go shut my door and turn on the television so they couldn't hear me cry in the pillow for poor little me. I know those nights of feeling lonely and sorry for myself and inadequate to handle my home and incapable of handling my job. I know those feelings, but I learned not to put them on my children.

I know of only three times in my life when I so completely fell apart that I didn't care if the kids saw me. And those three times they remember vividly. It hurt them. They felt responsible for me. Once I looked across the table and saw my daughter, with tears streaming down her face, looking at me.

"Oh mother, I'd gladly give my *life* for you," she sobbed. I had to ask the Lord's forgiveness.

Mothers, we have such a responsibility. Take your insecurities to God, take them to someone else, but don't take them to your children. They also are insecure, and if they don't find security in you, where are they going to go? That's what's wrong with a whole mixed-up generation of teenage kids. They went home with their insecurities, and they found parents who were more insecure than they were. Then they went to their peers, and said, "Hey, my old lady is really mixed up," and their peers nodded and said, "Mine, too." And then they got together, and the blind led the blind, and they all fell in the ditch. They clammed up and quit talking to us. Communication lines ceased— You know the story.

I'm not condemning. I don't believe in it. But if you've already blown it somewhere, get up and go on from here. Bring it to the Lord, confess that thing. "Lord, I have blown it royally with my kids. I've done this. I've done that. I've done the other thing." Then ask Him to redeem your mistakes, to help you do better. And He will.

It's not uncommon for women without husbands to sink down into such depression and self-pity, they say, "Don't talk to me about raising my kids. I just can't do it alone, and God knows it. Now, the whole thing is falling apart and I don't—"

But God keeps on saying, *I trust you with that child. I trust you to produce in that life an eternal appreciation for Me. I trust you to instruct him in the ways of righteousness. I trust you to impart to him the spirit of truth and the spirit of grace that I have imparted to you. I trust you to rise above your own problems, and give that child all that is due him because you gave him birth. Look up, and I'll help you.* And sure enough, He will.

We women without husbands are, in a measure, the headship of our children. My future son-in-law came to me and asked for Debbie's hand in marriage.

"Randy," I said, "I am thrilled that you're going to marry my daughter, but I want to ask you a question. I have been Debbie's headship for twenty years. I have covered her. When she hits her lows, I counsel her. When she hits her highs, I rejoice with her. I pray for her, for her protection, for her covering, for her guidance. I've asked God to take care of her. When she is not moving in faith, I have loaned my faith to her. When she marries you, I will transfer that responsibility and place to you. Are you willing to take it?"

Randy said, "Wow!" But he has done it. Beautifully. And they know it.

I am still in headship over a fifteen-year-old son. When the Lord called me to a traveling ministry, I put him in a Bible Academy in Oregon. He was willing to go to contribute to the ministry. I appreciate the unselfishness of a son like that.

Recently, I was in New York when a letter came to me. I ripped it open, and read, "Mom, we are having a parents' meeting this week. I know you can't come, but I wish you could." And then he underlined the words, "But I do understand. There are hungry hearts."

I couldn't help bawling, because his attitude is, "I will give my mother to the ministry, and my part of it is to stay out of trouble and get decent grades." It was particularly hard for him right then, because he'd injured his knee and was facing surgery. When I talked to him on the phone, I said, "Son, if this was a church and not a conference, honest, I'd cancel it and come."

He said, "Oh, you don't need to come, Mom. I'm okay. They're taking good care of me." It was good for him—and me.

If we exercise a proper headship and authority over our children, we teach them without having to say a whole lot of words. By our very lives we become an example of proper subjection and submission to authority.

The mother role is extremely important. In the chronicles of the kings of Judah and Israel, we sometimes find that so and so was a wicked king, who did evil in the sight of God "as did his mother." We find also that King so and so, the son of so and so, his mother, did right in the sight of God. The inference is that mothers exert a powerful influence on the lives of their children.

If you've had a child out of wedlock, and are still unmarried, you need to begin when the child is quite young to explain the situation to him. The simplest explanation is the best one. Opportunity often arises when someone asks your child about his father, and he comes to you with the question. You can explain, "You don't have a father, I don't have a husband, but God let you be born to me, and I love you."

As the child grows up and hears the moralistic approach, he might ask, "Mother, are you divorced?" When he is old enough to ask this question, he is ready to receive a fuller explanation. Then you can say, "No, I'm not divorced. I've never been married. A woman doesn't have to get married to have a child. If she sleeps with a man, they can have a child. It's not right, but mother did this. And I'm so glad I have you."

The child knows the facts and still feels loved. Somewhere down the line, somebody's going to say, "Hey, you're a bastard." It'll be painful to the child, but it won't destroy his confidence in you. The direct, honest approach will take away your otherwise constant fear that somebody might tell the child when you haven't prepared him for it. Speaking the costly truth in love is the least expensive formula for many of life's difficult situations.

Should you live with your children after they're married? Sometimes such an arrangement works out beautifully for all concerned. But not usually. Except in cases where it's unavoidable, it's better for you not to live with your children.

If you do have to live with your children, and are able to make some financial contribution to the welfare of the home, you ought to do it, even if it's a small amount. The attitude involved will be acceptable to your daughter and son-in-law, or son and daughter-in-law. Of course, if you must literally deprive yourself in order to pay them, they're not going to expect it from you. On the other hand, if money is relatively easy for you to come by, you must use a great deal of wisdom in being in their home.

Suppose your daughter and son-in-law, or the other way around, are using an old upright vacuum cleaner, and they're proud of it. Don't go out and buy them a tank type because you think they ought to have it. Don't buy them a color TV if their black and white suits them.

The principle here is, Don't usurp their rights. Don't come in and try to buy them out and set them up in the way you think they ought to live. Wait for the right moment—Christmas or a birthday—to do some things. Now, if they need something, or there's something you could contribute in the home without being an embarrassment to them, go ahead and do it. But be sure you approach it prayerfully, asking for wisdom.

Don't take your daughter on vacation because her husband can't afford to take her. Let the two of them be one in your eyes, just like the two of them are one in God's eyes. Take the attitude, "Because I'm in their home, I want it to be a better home."

Don't complain, "They're always using me for a babysitter." Set your limits and talk to them about it. Say, "There will be times when I'll be glad for you two to go away and leave me in charge of the children, but I'm not interested in devoting my life to taking care of them."

So that you don't feel guilty and they don't feel guilty, there should be a freedom. The attitude should be so unstrained and so free between you that they could say, "Hey something has come up," and you'd be glad to watch the children without feeling put upon.

But by the same token, don't let them take such advantage of you that you would be afraid to make plans to go out with a friend for fear they might need you at home.

I'll say it again: Except in cases where it's unavoidable, it's better for you *not* to live with your married children.

Let us not neglect our church meetings, as some people do, but encourage and warn each other.

(Hebrews 10:25 TLB)

9. You and the Church

In my encounters with pastors, ministers, and leaders of groups within the church, I do not find malice—"We're out to get the single woman. We're out to get the widows. We're out to get the divorcées"—but I do find a lot of woeful ignorance and unthinking prejudice. The institutional church doesn't quite know what to do with women who live in No Man's Land.

In the meantime, the problem is compounded by the fact that in the church today there is a lot of teaching centered on the family. Many of the big-name teaching tapes we're hearing, and many of the special sessions, seminars, and retreats we attend, have their major emphasis on the home. Discussions are centered on family life—husband, wife, and child relationships—and we singles have a tendency to feel we have been neglected, that there is no place for us in the church. Sometimes that feeling is confirmed by official action.

I heard recently of one minister who asked all his unmarried Sunday-school teachers to step down from their teaching positions. Then he filled the vacancies with married teachers, claiming his action was ordained of God. Singles in his church got the impression, "You don't have any sense if you're not married. You can't possibly know the mind of God. There's no way you can be a leader, a board member, a teacher."

A friend of mine reacted, "Wow! Jesus, Paul, and Lydia wouldn't have had a chance, would they?"

Once upon a time, the Catholic church went to the other extreme—only celibates could teach in the church. "You can't mind the things of the Lord if you're married," they said.

Neither of these extremes is the way of God.

I like to remember that Jesus' very closest friends were three unmarrieds—Mary, Martha, and Lazarus. Sometimes when Jesus wanted a reprieve from ministry, He went to their home. He went where He could rest, where He felt comfortable. His three friends understood Him. They didn't have to sit around and discuss the problems of getting along with their spouses or raising their children, because they didn't have any spouses or children.

In this day, I believe the Lord is reinstating an equally important place for singles in the church—as a matter of fact, He's had a place for us in His church all along.

One of the things which can delay the full acceptance of singles as singles in the church is a defensive attitude on our part.

Someone says, "We're going to have a banquet in the church—ten dollars a couple. We want everybody to come. We're all just going to get together, have a good time—"

Almost immediately, we singles stir up our martyr complexes to full production.

"Well, bless God, ten dollars a couple, huh? I suppose I've got to go out and get some guy to 'escort' me, or I can't even go to the banquet."

Hey! Wait a minute! Why don't you back up and go to the chairman and say, "Is this limited to couples?" And if it's not, say, "Mary, I've got ten bucks. Let's go—there's two of us." You might go and have a better time than anybody else. But if you don't say anything—if you just stay home and pout—nobody's even going to know you have a problem. Until six months later.

Then you may be in agony because of what happened. I can just hear you sobbing the whole story out to your pastor:

"Well, you know—sniff, sniff—six months ago when you had that banquet for couples—sniff, sniff—" You stop to rummage in your purse for another Kleenex, but you've used them all up already.

"Oh, my dear, that wasn't limited to couples," your pastor interrupts jovially, digging a freshly laundered handkerchief out of his hip pocket and handing it to you. "We had lots of singles there—and everybody had a ball!"

You don't know what to say then. You don't even know what to think. Wiping the water off your face, you blow your nose—embarrassingly loud—on his nice clean hankie and start crying harder than ever because you suddenly realize that all your bitterness has been for nothing. It'll take you a while to get over it, but maybe you've learned something.

Suppose there is a time when you ask, "Is this limited to couples?" and you're told, "Yes, it is." What then? Why, say, "God bless you. Hope you have a wonderful time!" and mean every word of it. Then scout around to find some couple that needs a babysitter and volunteer your services. That way, you can be a part of the success of the banquet.

Later, if "they" don't get around to dreaming up a banquet for singles, you can instigate one yourself. No need to be bitter about it. Couples just don't usually think in terms of singles, that's all. No reason why they should. Singles didn't plan the couples' banquet—couples don't need to plan the singles' banquet. You can do it—have it just like you want it. And maybe, when the couples get wind of what you're planning, they'll remember how you babysat for them, and they'll insist on baking some cakes and charcoaling some steaks for *your* party.

If we're bitter, grumbling, "The only ministry they ever want from us is babysitting, or teaching in the primary department," we've had it. It's up to us to show we can do something else, to be bold to witness, begin to share the reality we've found, not to bury our light under a bushel of bitterness and resentment.

We've got to begin to bless one another without feeling sorry for ourselves. I'm willing to give, because I know others are going to be willing to give—in a mutually satisfying relationship. We are always blessed as we submit to one another in love. It's guaranteed.

A lot of singles are leaving the church and meeting together on Sundays at some coffee shop where they feel wanted. Now, I'm one hundred percent for singles meeting together and fellowshiping. We need it, it's good for us—but not as a substitute for the church. The local church is absolutely vital to us for the covering it provides as well as for the teaching that comes through it.

When the minister gets up and speaks on the family again and again, we may wonder, "Man, what am I doing here?" The answer is that it's a chance for us to learn something. If we're in a particular church because the Lord has placed us there, He knows what He's bringing to us through His man or woman in the pulpit. And He knows that someplace, whether for our own life in the future or for some other life through us, we'll have an opportunity to use what we're hearing.

If Jesus Christ is Lord, He's Lord of that pastor, He's Lord of that Sunday-school teacher, and He's Lord over all our life. For us to say to the shepherd, or even to ourselves, bleating down deep inside, "I don't believe I'm getting the proper food here. I believe I'll go down the way to another pasture," is to invite trouble. Everybody knows that sheep get lost going from one field to the next one without a shepherd to guide them.

Your submission in your church is a key to safety. Go to your pastor, and commit yourself to his headship in spiritual matters. Say, "Pastor, I'm an unmarried woman, and I'm asking you to cover me spiritually."

Your pastor is over you in the things of God. And Hebrews 13:17 says we are to obey, to submit to, those who watch for our souls, so that when they give account, it will be with joy and not grief.

If you think you see something in the Word and you go to your pastor and he says you're out of line, you should listen to him and submit. Promise him, "Pastor, I will never say another word about it until you tell me different." Then you are free to hold the matter before the Lord and say, "Lord, if this is of You, You can reveal it to my pastor."

Suppose you have a burden for all the singles in the church, and you say, "Pastor, could we have a singles class?"

He says, "No way. We don't need a singles class. We need to all come together and fellowship."

You have not learned your lesson in submission if you say, "Bless God, I'll have it in my home, then." But if you say, "Thank you, Pastor. I submit to your authority, and I trust your walk with God. But I'm going to pray about this, because it's very important to me," you're in order. Then you can go home and get on your knees and ask God to change his mind.

I'm a great advocate of singles being used in the church, and I encourage pastors, saying, "Your singles need to learn submission, and since they don't have the opportunity of learning it in the bonds of matrimony, use them in the church. Let them learn submission as they're working with you."

Most pastors are willing to help, but if we come along with, "You're not telling *me* what to do!" it's easy to understand why they throw up their hands in disgust. "There! You see why we can't use singles? Too independent. They think they know all the answers. They're not teachable—too high and mighty. They want everything their own way—"

Let's be willing to learn some things. We've been so afraid everybody is going to take advantage of us that we've carried around the burden of a heavy defense mechanism. But the Lord says, *If you can make Me Lord, you don't have to defend yourself. I'll be your defense. In the church and everywhere else. You can just enjoy My peace.*

Many ministers are scared to death of a single female anyone—divorcée, widow, unmarried woman—coming to them for counsel. They dread it with a purple passion. Why? Because we demand from our ministers more than we're entitled to. Instead of coming to them for legitimate spiritual headship, we go to them as a replacement for the man we don't have. We want their attention, we want their guidance, we want them to tell us what to do with our lives—how to spend our money, how to get a better job, how to find a new apartment—the whole thing. And that's wrong! As singles, we have no right to say to our pastors, "Okay, I'm making you liable for my life." They hardly have time to run their own lives, much less take on ours.

We may go to our pastor for spiritual counsel, for enlightenment in the Word, for prayer for a special need. We may go to him for permission to set up a singles' program in the church. But we may not ask our pastor to take the place of the husband we don't have. It's our job to set the limit, to help him not to be afraid of us by not taking more from him than is right.

Ministers' wives often complain about the little unmarried someone who approaches their husband after every service—

"Pastor, please. I need to talk with you for just a teensy minute." Who could refuse so small a request? But the "teensy minute" invariably turns into at least an hour and a half, and the poor pastor doesn't get home until his dinner is cold and his family has dispersed to away-from-home activities.

And then there's the grass widow with the uncanny knack of telephoning with a million can't-wait problems—just when the preacher and his wife have crawled into bed. If thoughts could kill, her species would have died off long ago!

We shouldn't make ministers run away from us by being over-demanding. To be a blessing rather than a blight in the church, we've got to use wisdom.

But this one thing I do, forgetting those things which are behind, and reaching forth unto those things which are before, I press toward the mark for the prize of the high calling of God in Christ Jesus.

(Philippians 3:13–14)

10. Getting on with the Program—

Before you can get on with the program, you have to know what the program *is*—you have to know where you're going, what your goals are, what kind of growing you intend to do. Growing up is not easy—especially at our age—but it's vital if we're to go from one degree of glory to another, and that sounds so good to most of us, we're at least willing to try it.

Take inventory. What are your assets? Can you improve them? Don't say, "No, no way. I'm too old already." Remember Grandma Moses. At age eighty, she decided, "I think I'll improve myself." She started painting and became a famous painter.

Often in counseling, I've heard women say, "If I had someone to do it for—" That's a cop out. The Lord says, *You have you, and I'm watching you. Appreciate what I've given to you. Don't let it go to waste for lack of a big audience. I'll invite someone to look at what you've done and to applaud for an encore when I think you're ready to handle it.*

We need to improve our assets for our own sake, not for

someone else. It's a waste of time to sit back and wait to be discovered. And we have to have goals that are realistic, not like the goals of one gal I counseled recently.

"I wish I had a better job," she said rather wistfully.

"Well, you can get one," I encouraged her, eager to help. "What kind of work would you like to do?"

"I'd like to be a teacher." Somehow, she didn't sound very hopeful about it.

"Okay, what's your education?" I asked her, wanting to get down to the basics.

"Well, I graduated from high school, but I don't have any college—" Obviously, she had to get more education than she had if she wanted to be a teacher.

"Looks like your first step is to go to college, then, huh?"

"Well, but I can't do that. I don't have any money." She looked more mournful than ever.

"Borrow it!"

"But I'm forty-four years old. I don't want to borrow money and go to college." I began to suspect that she didn't really want anybody's help, either.

"You don't want to be a teacher, then," I told her bluntly. I should have been kind enough to tell her the rest of the brutal truth. What she really wanted, in her inmost heart, was to feel sorry for herself and have other people sympathize. Already, without half trying, she had reached her goal of self-pity.

Sure, self-pity is easy for us to achieve—but too expensive. It costs our whole lives—and we never have anything good or beautiful to show for all our down-at-the-mouth efforts. It's so much better to have a challenging vocational goal, one that gives us an interesting and fulfilling life as we go along. Self-pity—who needs it!

Be realistic about what you want to do with your life—get it out of the clouds. Don't live in a circle of broken dreams. "If only—" Deal with the realities life has presented to you. Here in the United States of America, we can do anything we want to do, almost. Really. It may take a while, and it may take a lot of effort. But if our goals are realistic, we can reach them.

Nobody else can set your goals for you. If they do, you probably won't reach them. You won't have the drive or the wherewithal or the faith to reach goals that are not really yours. Don't ask me what the goals for your life should be. I really don't know. But I believe *you* can know.

Set some goals you can attain this week. Have a short-range goal and a long-range goal. This way you are consistently accomplishing something. It makes a survival pattern, always something to be looking forward to, and it helps you accept yourself.

Sometimes I go to my room so tired, really exhausted after ministering. I'll be so worn out, I can't feel—I'll be almost numb. And I'll fall down on my bed ready to give it all up, it takes so much out of me. But while I'm lying there, the Lord will bring to my remembrance things that people have been saying—"Thank you, sister, the Lord just released me today." "Thank you, sister, the word really came forth from you." "Thank you, sister. Thank you." "Oh hallelujah! I received the Holy Spirit when you prayed for me." All these things will go through my mind, and I realize all over again that I am complete in Him.

Am I still a mother missing my kids? Of course! I almost bawl every time I see a teenage boy or a young girl in her twenties. I miss my two badly. But I feel complete because of what He does with His channel. And I am renewed. "Oh, God, thank You! Thank You so much!"

You can have completion and fulfillment—married or single—when you know you're in the center of God's will, when your goals for yourself are His goals for you.

How can you know that this is the will of God in Christ Jesus concerning you? If you're not in His will, you'll know it. Don't say, "I don't know if I'm in the will of God." His Word promises that *if* you are willing to do His will—that's the only catch—you'll *know* what it is (John 7:17).

Let your program, your goals, be realistically, prayerfully arrived at, and then set after them with all that's in you. Take literally the Scripture that says, "Work hard and cheerfully at all you do, just as though you were working for the Lord" (Col. 3:23 TLB) because you really are!

If you have to go back to school, go back to school. It's not four years out of your life, or two years out of your life. It's nothing *out* of your life—it's part *of* your life. Enjoy it. In everything, learn to find your enjoyment as you go along, leaving behind the waiting for that someday thing that never happens. The Lord has placed responsibility on you, and He has given you the ability with which to respond. He knows what you need—and He provides it.

If people who don't understand your real needs reach out and offer you pity, hand it back to them with a loud, "No thanks. I don't need any of that!" Pity will destroy you. Widows, divorcées, singles—all women without husbands (and all women with husbands)—ought to be scared of self-pity.

In II Kings 4:1–8 we read about a certain woman of the wives of the sons of the prophets. She must have been on the verge of self-pity at the hopelessness of her situation when she came to Elisha, saying, "Thy servant my husband is dead. And thou knowest that thy servant did fear the Lord; and now the creditor is coming to take my two sons to be slaves because of what my husband owed him."

And Elisha said unto her, "Okay, I heard your problem. What do you want me to do about it?"

"O Lord, I feel so lonely. God, I don't know which way to turn. My husband is gone, and now they want to take my boys, too." I can just hear her sobbing it out, can't you?

Well, Elisha listened, and when she had it all out of her system, he asked her another question, getting past the pity and down to the basics of a remedy for her trouble.

"What do you have in the house?"

She told him she didn't have a thing—except for an insignificant little pot of oil. She didn't think *that* would help any. Actually, she was so low she couldn't even recognize an asset when she saw one. But Elisha knew what God could do, and he told her to go borrow a lot of empty vessels from her neighbors and take them into her house, shut the door, and begin to pour out what she had.

Well, it sounded like such a foolish thing to do, but she was desperate, so instead of arguing with him about the foolishness of what he had asked her to do, she sent her sons out to borrow vessels. When they had come in, she shut the door, just as the prophet had instructed her to do, and began to pour her little pot of oil into the empty vessels. She poured and she poured. And she poured and she poured. Only when the last available vessel was full to the brim did her oil stop flowing. Amazing!

Then the man of God told her to sell the oil, pay the debtors, and live happily ever after with her children. Their every need could be supplied out of the money that was left over.

The same God lives today. And He can supply our needs out of the basic resources, the basic assets, that are already ours, if we will use them according to His directions.

When a woman becomes a divorcée or a widow, she might feel, at first, like the woman in II Kings 4—that she has mountainous debts and no resources worth mentioning. But as we are obedient to trust God, to pour out what He has given us, we find that He will supply all our needs in ways no less marvelous.

Our part is, first of all, to recognize the worth of what we are and have, and then to be willing to borrow from others the things we are lacking in ourselves.

It isn't easy for some of us. We've built up a little defense that says, "I'll never get hurt again," and we wall ourselves off from other people. Maybe we are a little bit defiant about it: "God trusted me to be alone. Okay, alone I'll be!" And we take our little hammers and drive nails in boards to build unclimbable walls all around us. It's a wonder we even hear when the Lord calls down, "You're going to starve to death in there."

"But Lord, all that I have is this little thimble full of oil. It can't last but *so* long."

"Well, how about getting out of that cage you're building to die in? Go visit your neighbors and see what you can borrow from them. Go out and let people bless you, let them benefit you, let them extend you. It won't just help you, it'll do them some good, too."

Iverna, I want to bless you with abundant life, not just a niggardly existence. How come you don't trust Me to supply a whole lot of blessings in your life?

He lets us ponder that one for a while, and then he pleads, so lovingly, *Iverna, don't be satisfied with so little. My Son died so that you could have everything. Don't let His dying go to waste.*

After we've gone out and borrowed what we could from the world, we have a responsibility to go back into our home with all we've borrowed and use it. The Lord says, *All right now, you've got your kids. Don't make anybody else responsible for how they turn out. I've capacitated you to take care of them—it's between you and Me. I'll be their father from now on. You just begin to pour out what I have given you. Let Me fill up all the increased capacity you have inside you. And out of the overflow, pour faith to My children. Pour blessing and anointing on your home.*

And as you are obedient to do what He says, you'll find suddenly that something's different. "O Lord! I don't feel the emptiness. I don't feel the loneliness, the hollowness, anymore. You've given me so much to be thankful for. I see abundance in my life! All my needs are being met above all I could have asked for. Hallelujah!"

And the blessings will keep flowing as long as we keep pouring them out.

This can be real in our lives. And nothing short of this oil from God's supply is going to pay our debts—our debts to society, our debts to the past, our debts to the future, our debts to the present. All those feelings of "I owe, I owe." You do owe, but what you owe is not to me—you owe it to the Lord.

"Lord, as I receive from You, I will pour out as unto You." The more I pour out, the more there is left. And as I'm giving and selling, as it were, all my own indebtedness is being paid,

55/26

because I'm giving forth the very oil that God has given to me.

It's a beautiful thing, the provision that the Lord has made. We don't have to sit back and say, "Oh, I'm just a taker. I'm on social security, and I take—" Garbage! Somebody paid the bill, and probably somebody you gave birth to. We're all paying it. And I'm delighted if any of you can collect it.

I'm serious about this. When that program falls apart, and there's no more money in that fund, we'll raise up another fund. I don't care if it's church-oriented or if it's social-oriented, because we're God's children. And He says, "I want you to have the best of both worlds."

We need to get off this little independent kick. If you have something coming, get it. If you're eligible, file. We're God's kids, and if we weren't here, the pagans wouldn't have a world fit to live in. They owe us something, just for being here. We don't need to lack anything.

When we have left off self-pity, and begun to get on with the program, we need to work out mechanisms for managing various relationships of our lives. What should we do about money, about friends, about employers, about God? Let's take a look at a few of these areas.

Singles have to have realistic financial goals.

I counsel so many people who say, "I am up to my neck in debt. I have to pay out $582 a month, and I get only $400." That is totally unrealistic. There's no way— You've got to do something different, extend some loans, or find a financial advisor who can tell you a better way to manage your money.

Married people are in debt, too. In many homes, husband and wife are both working, and they're still barely making ends meet. They've had to get their heads together and say,

"This is what we've got to pay. This is the way we're going to pay it."

Too many single people seem to have the attitude, "We should have all the advantages of married people and twice the fun." We run around together because nobody else wants us, and when we go into a restaurant, we laugh and say to each other, "Have anything you can afford." We need to begin to accept this as our way of life. If you drive a Mark IV, live in a penthouse, and all that, that's great. I'm happy for you—if you can afford it. If you live with somebody else in one room and cook on a burner in the corner, I'm happy for you—if that's what *you* can afford.

Live within your budget. If playing is important to you, budget money to play, and play without guilt. One thing that's important to me is to drive a nice car. That's not at all important to some people.

One of my friends couldn't care less. As long as her car runs, that's all she cares. She kicks it. She doesn't have a starter.

I ask, "How's your car?"

"My green Le Mans? Forget it, it's still running."

She doesn't care about a nice car. I spend money on a car, she spends money on other things that are more important to her.

Find out what's important to you, not what's important to your friends, your pastor, your leaders, or anybody else. What do you want to do? If you want to get your hair set every week, budget it and do it. If you don't, and you'd rather do your own, don't complain, "I wish I could get my hair done every week."

My brother Judson came to see me this Christmas. It was the first time he'd ever been to my apartment. He stepped in and looked around, and he said, "If I didn't know it, I'd know it by looking. This is you, sis." I'm a nester, although I travel all the time. My desire, the craving in me, is to be at home. I'm almost a stick-in-the-mud socially. My friends get mad at me because I'd rather be home than anywhere else.

I've fixed up my apartment just the way I want it. Piece by piece, I've bought exactly the kind of furnishings I like. It may sound dumb to you that I pay rent just to come home for three or four days a month, but it's important to me, more important than having that much money in the bank. I have a right to be me, and I know me. I know what makes me satisfied.

Because I travel around so much of the time, I carry with me a little vase with artificial flowers in it, and I have a tiny picture of the ocean. As soon as I get into my room, whether it's in a private home or a motel, I set out my vase of flowers, and I put my picture of the ocean alongside, and I say to me, "Welcome home." Might sound stupid, but it makes me feel good. I'm realistic about my needs.

One of the things we all need is human love and acceptance, and we need human attention. We need each other.

Our relationships with others involve giving and taking. One says, "I will give wherever I can, because as I give to you, I'm receiving from you your gratitude. As I give to you, I'm taking from you something that meets my own needs." That attitude helps you get along with other people. You are not then too vulnerable to their response to you. On a fifty-fifty basis, if you give me something, or do something for me, and I don't respond properly, you're hurt, and the whole thing snafus. But you can rise above that and say, "Iverna, in giving to you, I take a pleasure, a joy, a peace within that

says, 'I was able to give something to her, whether she liked it
or didn't like it, and I loved doing it.' " That way, we all win.

Give. Then take the joy of giving.

I see two classes of people in the world—pursuers and
people who are being pursued. Those who are pursued are
apparently liked by everybody. Everybody wants to be
around them. People are always asking them out. They never
learn what it is to have to reach out for friends. They can just
take their choice.

There is another class of people, the ones who do the
pursuing. And often, the people who are the pursuers resent
it.

"I'm *always* doing the asking—but I'm not gonna ask
anymore."

When you decide that, you're going to be lonely. You'll get
to sit at home with your pride.

"Bless God, I've still got my pride."

Good. I hope you enjoy it. It'll be your only company.

Or you can say, "I'm not the kind of person who is
pursued. I must pursue. I must reach out." And you'll have to
reach out to ten people, because eight will reject you. But so
what? If you can begin to see your role, not as a negative, just
as an interesting fact of life, you can begin to enjoy it. There's
no need to feel sorry for yourself and grumble about it,
groaning, "I'm not sought after. Nobody wants me. I'm
unlovely. Nobody likes me." These things are not necessarily
true. You're just your own unique personality.

People who are being pursued have their problems, too, a
different set of them. If you knew what they had to put up
with, maybe you wouldn't want to trade places.

If you have to do the pursuing, learn to keep reaching out

until you find somebody who can meet your needs and someone whose needs you can meet.

Women in No Man's Land seem especially vulnerable targets for other people's advice.

It's interesting how many of our friends take the liberty of approving or disapproving of our decisions merely because we don't have a husband. Of course, if we've involved them by asking advice, then we give them the right to judge. If however, we have asked opinions, weighed them, and then made our own decisions based on our own judgment, we should be mature enough not to be influenced by anyone's disapproval. Decisions have to be our own—we're the ones who will have to live with the consequences.

When you need advice, or need consolation or just someone to tell your troubles to, try to pick a mature Christian for a confidante—someone who will listen to you, pray with you, and someone whose fellowship will help you grow in faith. Ideally, you might choose someone who needs you to listen to her, too. That way you won't be taking, taking, taking without ever giving in return.

The single who chooses for her confidante a happily married woman with six kids, a full-time job away from home, a busy husband, and no household help, isn't being very considerate. Counsel that is grudgingly given while the pork chops burn, the mashed potatoes scorch, and the coffee over-perks is not likely to convey an abundance of blessing. If you *have* to ask advice of an extremely busy, involved person, be thoughtful enough to make an appointment that's convenient for them and edit your problem down to size before opening your mouth. Statement of a current problem shouldn't entail digging up details of the past ten years in a relationship. Be considerate of other people's time—and needs. Don't be a usurper, ever.

A word about our specialized need for the friendship of children: The need for motherhood is a drive within us from birth. Little girls play with dolls. We are mothers. Along with the ability to bear children, there came all the drives and emotions that go with motherhood. Don't feel bad about your maternal instinct. Don't fight it, and don't lie about it. Learn to express those instincts in acceptable ways.

You could do volunteer work in the pediatric ward of the hospital, give one day a month in the nursery, or you could babysit for your married friends. Don't bristle with the attitude, "I'm not going to be a babysitter for everyone just because I'm single." If your maternal instincts are strong and you're single, you can be a genuine blessing and help to strengthen families while you enjoy the hugging.

But from the beginning of the creation God made them male and female.

(Mark 10:6)

11. How to Get Out— of No Man's Land

How important is home to you? Do you enjoy being at home? Do you enjoy cooking? Do you enjoy fixing your home up, your apartment, your room? If you don't, be very slow to move toward marriage. Many women see marriage as Utopia, but they have no interest in housekeeping, and no interest in being at home. They don't enjoy entertaining in their home. They don't like to fix it up.

But suddenly some guy pops the question, "Will you marry me?" And all aflutter, like it's the wedding ceremony already, you say, "Oh, I do. I do. I do."

And when the knot's tied, and the honeymoon trip is over, he says, "Okay, honey, let's go home." And then you're home fifty-four years—washing dishes, hanging pictures, scrubbing floors—

Take a look at it. Know what you really want. If you do enjoy home, and something inside you says, "I wish I had a husband to enjoy it with," be honest with yourself. If you want to get married, you need to quit lying about it. Stop telling everybody, "I don't want to get married."

If you want a husband, it's nothing to be ashamed of. Marriage was God's idea to start with. In the beginning, He looked at man and said, *It's not good that man should be alone. I will make him an alter ego, another self. I'll make a helper fit for him, and they shall be one flesh,* and He created us. Women.

Then He said, *The woman shall be under the man.* So it is not wrong for us to say, "I want to be under a man." If that is realistically and honestly what we want, it's a normal and appropriate response created within us.

Before you start looking for a husband, ask yourself a few questions. Do you want a man of your own in order to bless his life, or for the pride of ownership? Do you want a man of your own because you feel that God has given you the capacity to bless him, to make him a better person than he could be without you, to bring joy and completion and fulfillment to him? Or do you want a man just so you can brag, "I've got a man of my own"? Honest answers to these questions will reveal *you* to *you.*

If you find you have a wrong motivation in seeking a man of your own, confess it to the Lord. "Lord, I've had a wrong motivation in this, and I give this to You." And if He brings you a right motivation, then, in faith, you can begin to pray, "Lord, bring the man into my life whose life I can bless and benefit, and the two shall be one, like You said. I will make him better by helping. Lord, prepare both of us for it."

If your motive is wrong, and the Lord doesn't give you a right one, forget about man-hunting.

But if the way is clear for you to go husband-hunting, you can pray, "Lord, I want to get married. I really do. I'm going to try to develop the capabilities You've given me. I'm going to try to be a better person, more attractive, more fulfilling, more considerate of others. Everything that You've placed in me, I will try to increase. Lord, I'm asking You to do in me a work which will equip me to be the beautiful balance to whomever You bring into my life. Thanks, Lord."

The Bible says that if we delight ourselves in the Lord, He will give us the desires of our hearts. I don't think that means He'll give us everything we think we want. But if He isn't going to give us what we think we want, He'll change our heart's desire, making us want the thing He intends to give us. And through it all, we'll know that He is Lord.

After we have prayed, we must be willing to take the man the Lord brings in our path. He may not look like what we had in mind. He may be bald instead of having black wavy hair. He may work in a dime store instead of owning a bank. But if we're in the Lord's will, and he's the man for us, we'll know it.

Everywhere I go, singles say to me, "Do you know any neat guys out there?"

And I say, "What's wrong? Don't you have any neat guys here?"

"Ugh!" they say. "You really ought to see them." We forget that if our goal is to help a man become everything God wants him to be, we shouldn't be looking for a finished product, but for raw material, someone we can help.

Years ago, there was a very dashing young man in our church. He had a lovely singing voice, wavy hair, and was always dressed *so* perfectly. Of course, he had a little wife, but— It was easy for us to forget that she existed. Every time he walked in, all the girls in the church nearly swooned. One day I mentioned him to my mother, concluding my description with, "Oh-h, I think he is *so* neat!"

"Iverna," she said to me, "who do you think taught him to

dress like that? Who do you think irons his shirt so smooth and makes sure his hankie sticks out of his pocket just so? Who do you think encourages him? When you see a man who walks like that—with a healthy ego and a confident assurance—you can know he's got a woman behind him who builds him up."

That was news to me, and as time went by, I forgot about it. Years later, there was a guy in our church who had dated just about every eligible girl, and we all had the same feeling about him. "So and so? Ugh! He's such a *creep*."

Then one day a girl moved into our community from another state. She didn't know he was a creep, and we didn't get to her in time to tell her. In nothing flat, she fell head over heels in love with the creep and they were married. Know what happened?

You guessed it!

He quit dragging his shoulders, quit wearing wrinkled old suits, quit looking so painfully self-conscious. All of a sudden, he was like an ad out of *Esquire*—starched white shirts, pants with knife-edge creases, and we all said, "Wow! I didn't know anybody could look *that* good!" But the little wife was sitting alongside of him, her hand lovingly and proudly resting on his arm, as if to say, "Sorry, girls. Too late."

If we're looking for the finished product, we can forget it. He already belongs to somebody else. If we want to get married, we must be willing to take the one God brings to us. And when we take our vows, we should look at him, head-on, and say, "I promise to love and honor and obey you till death do us part—not based on what I think you're going to become, but based on what you are now." And if that is our honest attitude, God will supply.

If God sets us free to look for a husband, we should begin to be the kind of person we want to find in others. I always ask, "Now, what kind of a guy would you like?"

"Well, you know, I don't really care. Whatever the Lord wants—just as long as he's tall and good-looking, a man of means, already has his education, knows where he's going. I don't want to raise someone out of the crib. Someone who will be a stronger Christian than I am, really grounded in the Word of God, somebody who loves children, who loves people, who is not overbearing, who's very gentle and tender—"

Jesus says, *Father, did We make any like that?*

We are to cultivate in ourselves the qualities we would like to find in a mate—to be just as attractive, just as intellectual, just as strong spiritually as we expect them to be. As we begin to improve ourselves, we can say, "Lord, this is what I would seek if I were looking, and so I think this is what others must be seeking when they're looking. Help me to become what someone is looking for."

A woman is responsible to bless and benefit any man she dates. If he is less than exciting, she can see an opportunity to minister to him. By the way she responds to him, she can make him feel more masculine and accepted by drawing him out in conversation, for example. The way she responds to his attention will make a difference in his total self-concept. If she laughs at his failures and takes for granted good things, she's not blessing him. But if she thanks him for opening the door and accepts it with the graciousness that she ought to, she's blessing him.

Sometimes women try to take more than has been offered to them. Men are wary of them, and rightly so. They say,

"I'm fearful of dating so and so. She's got claws." What they mean is that she's out to get a husband—or a pin or a ring, some kind of a commitment from him.

Dating shouldn't be a means to an end, but the end in itself. It's what we make of this night. It's what we make of this day, this opportunity to bless each other. If we'd approach dating with this thought in mind, then it wouldn't be a success or failure based on what we get out of it, but it would be a success or failure based on what we give to it.

It used to be that when a guy dated a divorcée or widow, he'd have in his mind, "She's hungry for sex." And so he approached her in a different way than he would have approached a sweet young thing. That difference has kind of fallen by the wayside because of all the promiscuity today. But we still have a little bit of this, more in the church than out of it.

Surprisingly, I hear of just about as many white-haired women encountering this problem as I do the younger girls. There are some old codgers who still think they're God's gift to women.

No matter how old or young we are, we have to be wise. I think we can tell the first time we're out with a man whether or not he has undercover activity on his mind. And we have a perfect right to say to him, "Look, Buster, let's get this thing cleared up right now. I'm interested only in your friendship, and if you're interested only in my friendship, fine. But let's not go out and spoil a beautiful friendship by fighting about sex. My mind's made up."

Maybe he'll apologize, and that'll be that. But if he doesn't, if he keeps trying to seduce you, I don't care how lonely you are, you are better off to let him go in another direction—not because I think you'll wind up in his bed, but because you'll end up hating yourself. What will go through your mind is something like this: *"That's* all he thinks I'm good for. *That's* the only thing he saw in me. He didn't want to talk with me, he didn't see any beauty in my fellowshiping. He just took me out because he wanted to go to bed with somebody." That realization is so devastating, so painful— Who wants it?

Because dating is a natural stepping-stone to marriage, we need to be prayerfully careful about whom we date.

The danger of dating a non-Christian is an obvious one. If you date him, you might fall in love. And if you fall in love with a non-Christian, you are headed for all kinds of trouble. I have counseled many wives who were reaping a harvest of sorrow because they married unbelievers. Because the guy wanted to marry the girl, he agreed to go through all the rites of the church, to say, "I do," but afterward, he said, "I'm not gonna go to church," and the heartache began.

There are always exceptions. I don't like hard-and-fast rules. There could be a rare time when the Lord specifically points your attention to a guy in order to lead him to know the Lord. Be careful and let Him guide you. As a general rule, no matter how scarce eligible Christian men are, you're better off without any man than to risk being unequally yoked with an unbeliever.

Another question that often arises for the Christian woman is, "What about getting married to a divorced man?"

There are some real negatives to this, but not as many as you've been taught. Let's look at some of the possible complications.

If the man has children and his ex is living, chances are nine out of ten that you're not going to be "mother." More likely, you'll be the dirty bird who married daddy. If the children are going to be in your home, and you're going to be responsible for them, you're setting yourself up for a position of giving, giving, giving, and not taking—for years. Some kids, after four, five, or six years, will come back and say, "I've really come to appreciate you," but at first—maybe forever—it's all give and no take, a thankless job.

Another thing to keep in mind is that this guy has already been one with somebody, and now you're somebody else he's going to be one with. No matter how great you are, you cannot shake him from some memories. He will inevitably make comparisons. Are you mature enough to handle this in your own mind without torturing yourself, wondering, "Is he thinking about her? Am I as good as she was?"

If you're mature enough to adjust, then perhaps you can bless his life and say, "I want to come in now, and I want you to be with me from this day forth. We two today will become one, and we'll move on together from this. And everyone who is a part of you—your children, your ex, your anybody else—I will do the best I can to be a blessing to them."

There are many good divorced men who have learned some things. We shouldn't shut our minds to them completely. But we have to be realistic and know there may be problems that will require real maturity from us. If we're immature, we'd better stay single—or marry someone just as immature as we are and grow up together.

Be certain that you have discussed and understand the scriptural premise for your marriage and can enter it in faith. Whatever is not of faith is sin.

It is not uncommon for a divorcée to be afraid of remarriage. We hear all the scary statistics about divorce, we listen to the problems our married friends are having, and our fear grows.

On top of all that, someone reads to us, like a final

commandment from which there is no appeal or reprieve: "And unto the married I [Paul] command, yet not I, but the Lord, Let not the wife depart from her husband: But and if she depart, let her remain unmarried, or be reconciled to her husband" (I Cor. 7:10–11). That's the last straw. We begin to quake in our boots for ever having ever remotely *considered* remarriage for ourselves.

It's time for us to put this Scripture right out in front of us and take a look at it, to be ostriches no longer. I'm sick to death of divorcées being mowed down by everybody's plow. I'm sick of the idea that because of a past mistake, divorcées must forever live in guilt and condemnation and loneliness.

This Scripture verse, like everything else that Jesus taught, is put there for our advantage, not to condemn us. Jesus dealt not with law, but with something much deeper than the law. He dealt with attitude.

In everything He taught, Jesus said, *You've been told, Thou shalt not, and I'm telling you that's over and done with. I came to fulfill the law, not saying "Thou shalt not do," but "Thou shalt not want to do."*

Back in the old days, on up to Jesus' time, it was a very common thing for a man to simply give his wife a writ of divorcement when she ceased to please him, for whatever reason. Before Moses gave them permission to do this, a man just threw his undesirable wife out of the house and took someone else in. In making provision for a writ of divorcement, Moses set the woman free to marry someone else.

When Jesus came along, He said, "Because of the hardness of your hearts, because you had no right attitudes at all, Moses set this law for you, to give some protection to women." A woman might have given her best years to her husband, and all of a sudden, he found a cute little gal around the corner and threw his wife out. She didn't know what to do. There were usually only two alternatives open to her—she could sell her body or she could starve to death. So Moses set up the bill of divorcement, permitting her to remarry if she could find someone who'd have her.

When Jesus came along, He said, "Your attitude toward this whole thing is wrong. Marriage is ordained and instituted by God, and you're ignoring His whole idea by dealing with it from a selfish and often sensual perspective. All you want is someone to please you. That's typical of the natural man, but wholly inappropriate for those who have been called to live in the kingdom of God."

For us to get married with the loose attitude, "If it works, it works, and if it doesn't work, I'll try again," is to have the attitude of the unbeliever.

The Lord said, "That's not true of My church, My people. When My people come into the bonds of matrimony, they should see it as sacred, and they will realize there may be hard places for them, but the two of them shall be one. Any other attitude is adulterous in nature."

But what happens when you marry and don't make it? Maybe you didn't know how to make it. I surely didn't. I was about as wise as a dove and harmless as a serpent— I had it all mixed up.

I married a man when I was in a backslidden condition, and while he was overseas, I bore a child and gave my heart back to the Lord. When my husband came home, I had about as much wisdom as would fit into a thimble. I sat him down and said, "Now, listen here. Let me tell you how things are going to be. We will no longer do this and that and the other thing. You're not going to smoke in my house, because this is God's house. Don't put your beer in my refrigerator. This house is dedicated to the Lord. I won't stand for those things now, and I'm not going to raise our child in that kind of atmosphere."

Another child and ten rocky years later, he said, "Goodbye, Iverna. I'm going to find somebody I can live with." He did, they were married, and they've lived happily ever after.

What happens in a situation like this, when we didn't know some of the things we should have, and we are already divorced? Are we in a category of unpardonable sin which says, "Too late for you. Live alone all your life. You can never have a rightful place in the church, because they don't want you. Maybe you can move away and hide it so nobody will ever find out. But don't fill out any application blanks, because they might ask for your marital status."

I believe that Jesus told us what our attitude should be when He said, "Please, if you are going to get married, get married with the understanding that God sees the two of you as one. You are united. And if you would disunite from one man and go live with another man, it is adultery in the sight of God."

All of us have to start from where we are. "Art thou loosed? All right. Begin where you are," Paul said. "Don't start over again on the wrong foot."

A great tragedy I find often is that a woman is divorced from a man, he has married another woman, and all of a sudden the first woman meets the Lord. Then somebody comes along and says, "You're *really* his wife." And so she sits at home waiting for him to divorce his second wife and remarry her. That thing is as godless as it can be.

When my husband divorced me and married another woman, he died to me—except as the father of our children. It was final.

There is no bitterness left. There are no pangs of desire left, either. I'm not looking at him and longing. That thing is over. Am I bound by the law? No. I'm no more bound by that law than I'm bound by any other law in the Word.

Are you under the law? If you're under the law, you're already guilty, because you can't keep the law. I'm in Christ, and I believe that even the Church now is beginning to take another look at this and see it as an individual thing. The Bible says whatsoever is not of faith is sin. If you cannot by faith, remarry, then for Jesus' sake, don't. Don't go to anyone and have them talk you into it. Find the answer to that thing between you and God, and whatever you decide, don't let somebody else put you down in guilt.

Everywhere, the Lord taught balance. He opened avenues to abundant life, He didn't slam doors on it. Sometimes it would be a greater sin for a personality not to remarry than it would be to remarry.

I don't pretend to have the answer for you. God does. There are some really good books on this subject, but again, don't try to find a book to convince you. Please say, "Lord, thank You that You've released me from all my past. I am going on in Christ from this point on. You're my Lord."

People often ask me, "Do you think you'll ever remarry?" No, I don't think I will, but if the Lord brought someone into my life, and I knew it was of God, I'd be free to do as He led me—because He's my Lord and Master, and He knows what's right for me. I'm relaxed in that—but like other divorcées, I've got battle scars. I've been badgered from hither to yon by people who didn't know any better.

When you go to a pastor, and you say, "Pastor, I'm divorced. Can I remarry?" what do you expect him to do? The only thing that he can do is read you the Scripture verses. He doesn't know the answer either. And then you think, "Well, my pastor says if I ever remarried, I would be living in adultery."

In Revelation 21, we read, "All liars shall have their part in the lake which burneth in fire and brimstone." How many of you never told a lie? We take one little area such as the one about divorce and remarriage, and we make it a rigidity— then we take another little area such as lying, and we say, "Well, but—"

If we are marrying in the will of the Lord, we need not fear. And it isn't because *we* are special that our marriage will work when no one else's seems to. It's because *He's* special, our Lord. And if He brings someone into our life and says, "This man is for you. I want the two of you to reflect Me to one another," it's going to be a beautiful thing.

When I was a little girl in Sunday school, they used to talk about martyrdom, about how the soldiers would clomp in wearing their shiny boots and say, "If you don't denounce the Lord Jesus Christ, we're going to cut your head off."

Our teacher would say, "How many of you this morning promise—"

Oh, I'd want to promise my complete devotion to Jesus, but mentally, I'd hear the soldiers coming, and I'd hear myself shouting, "Jesus, I denounce You!"

There's no way any of us can muster up martyr faith now, on our own. Martyr faith isn't self-induced, and God doesn't give it until it's needed. But I'm convinced that if the soldiers were really on the way to arrest me, martyr faith would take over.

I'd say, "It's okay, God. I believe that Jesus' grace is sufficient for me."

In the same way, His grace would be sufficient for you in a remarriage situation. But there's no need for Him to give that grace to you until you need it.

What should you do about reinstating your marriage if your husband does not know the Lord? This is where faith is demanded on your part, faith to know that if the Lord wants the marriage reinstated, He will bring the man to know the Lord. You'd be most unwise to remarry him first, lest you have to repeat the whole painful, painful thing all over again.

I *know* you're lonely. I know what you feel like when the sun goes down. Before my ex remarried, I reached for the phone lots of times. I wanted to call him up and say, "All is forgiven. I'll meet you at such and such a place."

Then the Lord would say to me, *Iverna, what makes you think things will be different this time? Your incompatibilities are still there. Would you really be willing to do all the things he wants you to do? Would you be willing to give up Me?*

I'd say, "Oh, no, Lord!" and I'd take my hand off the phone. And by morning, I'd be intelligent again. But when the sun goes down, my heart comes up and takes over. You learn to guard against these things. And you pray daily, "Lord, I'm willing to go back to him, but You said, 'not an unequal yoking.'" Then you keep on praying for His salvation.

Our whole attitude—in everything—should be, "Lord, I'm striving to please You. You are my Master. You are my Lord."

Fear not, for you shall not be ashamed; neither be confounded and depressed; . . . you shall not [seriously] remember the reproach of your widowhood any more. For your Maker is your husband, the Lord of hosts is His name.

(Isaiah 54:4–5 TAB)

12. You and God—

Ultimately, the key to happiness in No Man's Land—and everywhere else—isn't in anything as relatively superficial and one-sided as how well we handle our finances, our careers, our friendships with other people, or our children, but in our relationship to God.

The Bible says that the unmarried woman cares for the things of the Lord, that she may be holy both in body and in spirit. And if we're to be truly happy in No Man's Land, we have to care for the things of the Lord. And in order to care for them, we have to know what the things of the Lord *are*. We find that out as we get to know God, the same way we get to know anybody else, by spending some time with Him.

It isn't easy. Satan knows that if we get to know God, he'll lose us for hell, and so he operates accordingly. He's pretty successful, too, at getting people to do everything *but* pray or praise God or simply *be with* the Lord. We'll serve on committees, we'll telephone shut-ins, we'll visit new members, we'll make potholders—we'll do any dumb thing in order to put off spending time with the Lord. And we suffer when we neglect Him, we really do. It's more important for us, in our position, to know the Lord than it is for us to do anything else. We *need* to know Him.

One of the ways we get to know God is by reading His Word. He reveals Himself in His Word.

Iverna, here's a book of sixty-six letters. Start reading them—and take them very personally, because I wrote them just to you.

A long time ago, I began reading the Bible with a strictly personal approach. I'd pick it up and say, "Lord, thank You for writing to me tonight. I appreciate it. What are You saying to me?" When I began to give Him my attention, He began to reveal His word to me, and all of a sudden, my needs began to be met.

I talk to Him—He hears me. He talks to me—I hear Him. I really began to get acquainted with God when my prayers became a two-way street. Listening to what He has to say to me is a whole lot more interesting than just telling Him what He already knows.

Real prayer is very therapeutic. There are a lot of us who need to get a lot of garbage out of our systems, things we've been suppressing in our subconscious. We're like a bunch of pressure cookers, just sitting there on the stove at first, building up pressure inside. Every once in a while, the pressure gauge jiggles and we go "Ps-s-s-t." It's quite harmless. Letting off a little bit of steam from time to time is essential for our survival in the world—and for the world's survival with us in it.

Telling God our troubles in prayer, and listening to His suggestions, is a perfect way to keep the pressure relieved and under control. The alternative is to suppress and suppress and suppress—like a cooker whose valve is stuck shut—and suddenly, without warning, BOOM! all over the ceiling. The whole thing blows up in everybody's face—and somebody invariably gets hurt—we more than anybody else. While they pick up the pieces, people shake their heads and say, "Man, I don't understand what happened to her. I thought she was such a lovely Christian."

I understand what happened to her. She didn't take it to the Lord in prayer. She was a professional suppresser. Every time somebody hurt her, every time somebody crossed her, she just crammed it down into her pressure cooker and said, "I don't care. It doesn't make any difference to me. I'm not hurt. I could care less."

She lied. She *did* care, it *did* make a difference to her, and she hurt like crazy. When it got so bad she couldn't stand it anymore, she cried out, "O my God, I can't take any more!" God heard her, and loving her, tightened the lid.

Why would He do such a cruel thing? To help her. He doesn't want His people to be living above and around and underneath reality. He wants us to be open before Him. He wants us to trade our rusty old shackles for a glorious new song, a song of freedom. And so He gives us more than we can stand so we'll finally give it all to Him—and let Him stand everything *for* us.

When we begin to spend some time with God, getting to know Him and getting just a little whiff of how much He loves us, we're on the road to contentment.

We all know what it is to meet a guy about our own age and feel that certain magical something between us. Man, that's excitement! He takes precedence over everything else. He's all we talk about, and all our friends hate us because of it.

"Did I tell you what Dick said the other night?"

"No, and please don't tell me. I don't want to hear about him. I'm jealous."

They try to turn us off, but nothing dampens our enthusiasm. We get in bed at night and try to go to sleep—and we see him. Day and night, our mind stays fixed on him. We can't help it. It's how we're made.

Do you know that we can get just as excited about the Lord? That's not superspirituality. That's reality. He says, *Behold, I will do a new thing,* and He does. He keeps on doing new things. I never cease to be amazed.

I say, "God, You're so cool—what are You going to do next?" He doesn't ever do what I think He's going to do. He always surprises me—does something better, way above what I've expected or asked for.

Every once in a while, I used to say, "I think I'll test Him—to see if He really does love me." I'd do something naughty—and then I'd wait, daring Him.

"All right, God. Withdraw Your anointing. Cause me to get fired from my job. I don't care. Just do whatever You want."

I would stand there, with my arms folded, acting spunky, and I couldn't believe my ears. I'd hear Him saying, *Oh, Iverna, I love you so much.*

"God! How can You say You love me? You know the bad thing I've just done—on purpose, too."

But God still smiled on me. He said, *My banner over you is love. I just can't help loving you. How I look forward to your coming to Me every day, just to spend time with Me. I save things to tell you during those very specific moments when I know you're listening. And I've got the neatest thing to tell you today.*

Writing to the Ephesians, Paul expressed an interesting

hope when he said, "May your roots go down deep into the soil of God's marvelous love, and may you be able to feel and understand, as all God's children should, how long, how wide, how deep, and how high his love really is, and to experience this love for yourselves, though it is so great that you will never see the end of it or fully know or understand it" (Eph. 3:17–19 TLB). Paul is saying he wants us to know God's love, but that His love is really so big we might as well give up, because we can never know it all. It's just too much—

In His Word, God tells us a lot about this love which is too vast, too deep, for us to know it completely. He says, *Herein is love, not that you've loved Me, but that I have loved you.* The Lord goes on to say, *I know, Iverna, that you didn't love Me first. Your mother taught you to love Me, but you still saw Me as a cop. You still see Me a lot of times as someone who will quit loving you if you do wrong. But I'm going to teach you about My love—it's different from the love of man. Why, man's love is just the faintest echo of My love.*

Iverna, I love you so much that I have given Myself for you!

I was almost shocked by the specific-ness of what He revealed to me, and I understood, better than I ever had before, that He didn't just give Himself for everybody, He gave Himself for *me*. If I generalize the Word of God, it can never have the depth of meaning to me that it's supposed to have. The Word was Spirit-inspired, and it's intimate and personal to me, part of a love relationship.

When we begin to understand just a tiny part of how much God loves us, it's easy to make Him Lord of our life, the boss of all of it.

What does He want? What does my Lord want in my life?

These questions, involved with seeking His will for me, are quite different from the things I used to ask in my prayers. The old prayers went something like this:

"Lord, I'm coming to You now in the name of Jesus. You said whatsoever things I asked in Your name, in faith believing, I could have. Well, here's my list. You better do it. You've got twenty-four hours to prove Yourself."

But now, my new prayer *had* to be, "Lord, be the Lord of Iverna. Here are the reins of my life. From now on, You guide me. Don't let me boss You around anymore."

In surrendering all to Him, I didn't take a step of defeat, but one of glorious victory. From that point on, I was ready to trust God to guide me in everything.

In the New Testament, we see how Jesus called the people unto Him—"Come unto me, all ye that labor and are heavy laden." He healed them, and then He taught them. Jesus does the same thing all through our lives. He calls us, heals us, teaches us one thing, and then He says, *Come up higher. I want to teach you something else.*

Think back to your highest spiritual time, your mountain-top experience with the Lord. Maybe it was when you first met the Lord, when you were baptized in water, or when you were filled with the Spirit. There is someplace in your life that was your spiritual utopia. Did you know that that highest point was meant to be your lowest point? You are never supposed to fall back from there. When you have put yourself back there mentally, listen to the words that Paul is speaking: "Stand fast right there. Don't waver. Don't backslide. Be steadfast, immovable."

We are to stand fast at the highest, most mature, most spiritual time of our lives, because if we don't stand fast there, we'll never go beyond that point, and the Lord wants to increase in us.

The Word of God teaches that it's possible for Him to increase in us, for us to be changed from one degree of glory to another as we look at Him—if we stand fast, never lose ground. And eventually we'll arrive at a fantastic pinnacle: "When he comes we will be like him, as a result of seeing him as he really is!" (I John 3:2 TLB).

Inevitably, the first thing that will happen to us after we have decided to stand fast is that the devil will threaten us.

One time, I had been speaking in New Jersey, Washington, D.C., and in New York. Things had been going along fine—God was moving and blessing. Then, all of a sudden, for no discernible reason, I felt myself going down, down, down.

I couldn't understand it. No one had done anything to me. There were no negatives in my life that I knew of. I never had it so good. God had been blessing in a glorious way. But all at once, the light, the joy, were gone. It was unbearable. I couldn't stand it.

"O God, I don't know why I'm here. Why did You put me in the ministry? Here I am, poor little kid, a million miles from home—" Self-pity was piling deeper and deeper. I was about to drown in it.

I went to my room and tried to pray, to rise above it. "After all," I reminded myself, "you're a teacher. You're out there ministering the Word, telling everybody that when they start to go down, the first thing they should do is to praise the Lord, and they'll automatically bounce right back up again." I decided to try my own advice.

Pacing the floor, I said, "Praise You, Lord. I just praise You. Hallelujah. I just thank You for this wonderful opportunity to prove You. Glory to God." The words rolled out like tires with no air in them. Instead of bouncing back up, my spirit dug deeper into the gravel, just like a flat tire.

Finally, I gave up, took a bath, and dragged myself to bed.

In the night, I dreamed that I was screaming, "O God, have mercy on me and protect me from this thing." I woke up dripping with perspiration even though it was nearly zero degrees outside. Suddenly, I knew what was happening. "For we wrestle not against flesh and blood, but against principalities, against powers, against the rulers of the darkness of this world, against spiritual wickedness in high places" (Eph. 6:12). That awareness made me determined to keep on fighting until I had the victory. I couldn't give up—I didn't dare.

As I lay in my bed, I said, "Hallelujah! I'm glad it happened. Now I'm mad! Lord, Hallelujah!"

I don't know how long I prayed before I fell asleep—with the victory.

The next day, I got a phone call from a friend in California. She said, "Iverna, are you all right?" When I assured her I was, she explained, "Last night, the Lord spoke to me, and I heard your voice screaming out, so I fell on my face before the Lord and interceded for you."

Wow! Was I ever glad to have a friend who would pray for me! Over the years, I have had to learn how to stand fast in all the Lord has done for me. Looking back, I can see five basic attitudes I've learned that have helped me stand fast in the peace and joy He's given me in the very midst of No Man's Land.

1) Resist anxiety. Be careful for nothing. Jesus taught the same thing when He said, *Don't worry about tomorrow. Don't think about it; tomorrow can worry about itself. Today has got enough to worry about.*

One day I was driving along and the Lord said to me (I don't hear voices, but when something comes to my mind that is smarter than I am, I always know it's the Lord), *Iverna, the main thing wrong with today is the fear of tomorrow.*

I thought back over my life, and I've had some struggles, some sicknesses, a divorce, some problems, some real complexities in business, and so on. However, under God, there has never been one day that was unbearable. But worry about what was going to happen the next day has almost killed me more times than I could count.

2) Learn to make all your requests with thanksgiving. When we do that, we are declaring our faith. The best definition of faith I've ever heard is, "Faith is when heart and mouth agree." When my heart agrees with my mouth on positive declarations, faith is sealed. As I make my request known with thanksgiving, "Lord, work in me, and I thank You that You will," I'm opening a channel of faith to Him, and He is able to pour back into me through that channel. It's open, expecting something, not clogged shut so the blessing can't get through.

3) Be ruled with peace. Psalm 119:165 says, "Great peace have they which love thy law; and nothing shall offend them." How well the Lord takes care of us! If we love His law and are obedient to resist anxiety and make our requests with thanksgiving, the God of peace rules our hearts and minds through Jesus Christ.

Here's the storm; here are the boats; here are the disciples; and here's Jesus. Jesus said, *I'm ruled with peace. Goodnight,* and He went to sleep.

Here are the disciples in the same storm, the same boat, but their faith wasn't up to His. They didn't sleep. They worried.

"Doesn't He know the problem? Let's wake Him up to tell Him the problem."

We have to learn to be ruled with peace. "Lord, I know You're somewhere in this storm. I can't see You right now, but Your Word tells me that You're in everything. Your Word tells me You'll never let me go through anything alone. You'll never leave me. Please help me to see You in this. Goodnight, Lord. Amen."

Have you ever been in your home, and for some unexplained reason, the whole atmosphere was conflict? I'm not talking about fights or arguments, I'm talking about the atmosphere. It's not peaceful. It's turmoil, frustration. Do you know that you can literally wield the weapon of praise against that and bring peace into your home? I've done it hundreds of times, just praising the Lord. "Hallelujah, Lord! I praise You. I don't know the problem, so I can't pray. I don't know what caused it—it's just here. Praise You, Jesus."

One morning I got up, and my house felt like there were no lights on—but they were on. Have you ever had that feeling? You just felt dark?

I wasn't sure whether it was Iverna or the situation, so I poured a cup of coffee and looked around again after I'd "come to" for the day. Everything was still gray, and it puzzled me.

I went into my bedroom to get dressed for work, and the Holy Spirit said to me, *Are you going to let this happen?*

I sputtered indignantly. "No, no I'm not, now that You mention it." And I began to praise the Lord. It was just as if someone had turned a floodlight on in my bedroom, the change was so remarkable. I walked through my entire house praising, praising the King who's coming, and I saw His light fill every corner! By the time I had finished, I felt like a woman of power in a kingdom of light.

God dwells in the praises of His people, and in Him there is no darkness at all.

4) Learn to regulate your thoughts. The Scripture lays it out explicitly: If there be anything lovely—of good report, if there be any virtue—think on these things. How can we do it when our news media are full of uglies, negatives, and bad reports about everything? We can rejoice in God's promise to work all things—good and bad—together for good for those who love Him.

The Bible says that when we begin to see these things begin to pass, we should lift up our heads and rejoice, because there's coming a redemption, a restoration— Sometimes I feel the waves of it, and I see something. There's coming a latter day, and it's far more glorious than anything we've ever seen. Knowing that, I can't help being joyful.

5) Lastly, respond to good teaching. Paul says that we are to *do* the things we've heard him teach and seen him do. If we don't act on what we've learned, the teaching can't benefit us.

Multitudes came to hear Jesus. They delighted in the things He said—but very few practiced them. The disciples said, "We want to know more." But they didn't always follow what they had already been taught. And there came a day when they all ran away.

It's one thing to hear, but if we specialize in getting excited about hearing a lot of things and remain hearers only, the teaching dies in us. It bears no fruit in our life. And there'll come a day of accounting when the Lord will say, *Those things you heard, and those things you saw, you didn't do.* We'll share His sorrow at our failure.

Begin now to appropriate in your own life the Word of God, that you may be joyful, that you may know His happiness anywhere—yes, especially in the midst of No Man's Land.

Fi

> *Delight thyself also in the Lord; and he shall give thee the desires of thine heart. Commit thy way unto the Lord; trust also in him; and he shall bring it to pass.*
>
> (Psalm 37:4–5)